MW01088663

The SECRETS of LIFE and DEATH

ANSWERS FOR YOUR JOURNEY
THROUGH THIS LIFE AND BEYOND

Richard G. Shear, Ed. D.

Copyright © 2011 Richard G. Shear, Ed. D.
All rights reserved.
ISBN: 1461086426
ISBN 13: 9781461086420
Library of Congress Control Number: 2011905846

Edited by William Loob and David R. Shear

I know this world is ruled by infinite intelligence. Everything that surrounds us— everything that exists—proves that there are infinite laws behind it. There can be no denying this fact. It is mathematical in its precision.

—Thomas A. Edison

This book is dedicated to all those who are seeking answers to why our world is the way it is and how to make it better.

Contents

What Are The Secrets of Life and Death

There is an old curse that states, "May you live in interesting times." In the same mindset is the realization that inquisitive people are cursed. This occurs because insight and understanding can sometimes drive us crazy. The more we understand, the more questions we have. This type of mind eventually reaches a state in which answers are elusive and out of reach. Somehow we come to the realization that the answers to life's great questions are veiled as a mysterious secret.

We are told by religious groups, scientists, philosophers and others that the inquisitive among us must wait to find out about the great secrets of life. The fact is that simply is not true. This book has been designed in a format to reveal answers to questions that probe the secrets of life and death, one secret at a time.

My search for meaning centered on three crucial questions. If we had the answers to these three questions, our stay on Earth would make sense and we would be able to understand why the world is the way it is. We would be able to understand why evil exists and why, for many, life is such a painful experience. We would better understand the concept of death and its relationship to life. Perhaps most important of all, we would understand how to make each day joyful, meaningful, and peaceful.

The first great question is, *What happens to us when we die?* As we live our lives, we always know that our own life and the lives of our loved ones is a temporary existence. Each one of us knows that we are just passing through this lifetime, and we never know how long our stay on Earth is destined to be. Given this difficult backdrop, I believe we would live in much greater comfort if we had proof that everything will be all right when we pass away. We want to know that upon death we transition to the other side and that our existence continues. It would help to know that we reunite with loved ones in a world that has left pain behind.

The second great question is, *Why are we here?* All of us, at one time or another in our lives, look for meaning in our existence. Is our time in this world a test? Can we ever know while we are alive, why God created Earth and put humankind here? Is there something special God wants us to do during our stay on Earth? What does God truly expect of us as we face the challenges of our lifetime?

Which leaves the third great question, *Are there things we can do to make our stay on Earth better?* Life is frequently a maddening, unkind time for our souls. We are surrounded by temptations to do the wrong thing in a world that seems constantly out of order. Is there a way to learn the tricks of living our lives that would make our stay on Earth more special and loving?

This book is written in three parts, each focusing on one of the three crucial questions. Although the book is designed in this manner to add clarity, it is important to understand that our existence is aligned with a single thread. What happens when we die, why we are here, and tips on living our life are all parts of the greater whole.

Understanding what happens when we die frames how we should live. How we should live is made clear by an understanding of why we are on Earth. Everything that happens in our existence makes sense and is a byproduct of the connectedness of all things.

Secrets are forms of discovery. They are answers to questions we were led to believe would not be answered during our lifetime. Death is wrongly defined as an end. It is a doorway transitioning our soul to another vibrational state that we live in. We never die, we always live, but for clarification of terms and as used in this book, life is best defined as our time on Earth.

God, the creator, or the universe are all interchangeable terms for the same force. Whether we understand it as God, the creator, or the universe, it is the creative force that is responsible for our existence. We spend our time trying to fathom God and we do it in human terms. God has been referred to as vengeful or jealous, and ascribed other human qualities that are better applied to the behavior of humans on Earth. The creative force is best defined as pure love. The universe has put us on Earth at this time to learn, and the lessons will unfold, page by page in *The Secrets of Life and Death*.

    The Secrets of Life and Death is about showing how God does allow us to see the answers. There is a reason why we are here, there is an expectation of what we are to do, there are ways to make life better, and there is proof of what happens to us when we die.

Why I Searched for the Secrets of Life and Death

I would like to have written this book from a dispassionate, academic viewpoint. But that was not to be my role in this lifetime. In 1992, momentous, life-changing personal experiences turned my quest for answers to the meaning of life and death from a mere intellectual curiosity to a driving passion. Over the years since then, I have asked the crucial questions about life and death as much to help others find comfort as to find answers myself. This book is, in a way, a compendium of that journey.

I suppose people would say that I have lived a pretty traditional life. I am an award-winning educator. I have served as the principal at three high schools, as well as an assistant superintendent of curriculum and instruction. I was the first person to be recognized in my home county as The County Teacher of the Year. On a more fundamental, personal level, I am the father of a miracle son who fought back from a low birth weight of 17 ounces to become an incredible young man. The people who were part of my world in 1992 know the other side of that story: I am also a father who lost one of his twin sons.

In my work life as a school leader, I have supervised the education of thousands of young people and dealt with both the mundane and the extraordinary. As a high school principal, I have had incredibly wonderful moments, but I have also investigated murders, dealt with child abuse, and have had more than my fair share of dealings with borderline personalities. At one point, I would have thought that the totality of my experiences would have prepared me for anything that life could throw at me. However, nothing in my lifetime had prepared me for the life changing, unexplained event that was to happen. Simply stated, on more than one occasion, I received conclusive, irrefutable contact from a son who passed away at birth. He was not only giving me proof that his consciousness had survived death, he was also sending me a message of love and comfort.

The journey of discovery that unfolds in *The Secrets of Life and Death* starts with taking up the concept that we do not die at the end of our earthbound lives. However, proving that our consciousness survives death, is only one part of the story. It has been the challenge of human beings throughout history to understand ourselves as well as our existence. Knowing that death is inevitable, we wonder what really happens to our soul when we die. As thinking, reflective beings, we also want to know why we are on Earth in the first place. We want to know more about God's plan for us and what he wants us to do and learn during our lifetime. Additionally, because our daily existence is often a struggle, we are seeking methods to make our lives easier. *The Secrets of Life and Death* provides answers to the questions of our existence. It is a road map designed to provide answers that will make your life more meaningful, joyful and peaceful.

My journey to find the answers to the big questions of life and death has been a lifelong pursuit. I grew up on Long Island the youngest son of two hardworking people. My father was a war hero who came out of World War II with a wife and son and no time to go back to engineering school. He subsequently spent his life as a butcher. He did very well in his career through the mid-1950s as he managed his own store in Yonkers, New York. However, a new invention called the supermarket sent that dream crashing, and he spent the rest of his career working in an icebox for the A&P. Still, during my teenage years I remember my father as being pretty optimistic. Certainly, his life experience had helped shape his approach to each day. At age twenty, he landed on the beaches of Normandy with over 150 men. A year later he and one other soldier from that landing were the only ones who had not been killed, maimed or become a POW. As would most people, at one time I would have considered my father's survival through some of the most horrific battles of World War II as good fortune. Today, my research into the questions of life and death has taught me that his survival had much less to do with good fortune than it did with his karmic destiny, that being: we are all placed on Earth so that our souls can gain knowledge.

There was a reason why his soul determined that he would not die in World War II. Every person he encountered from that point on has had a different life because he did not die on the battlefields of France and Germany.

My mother was an exceptionally good person who probably should have spent her life as a baby nurse. Instead, as a result of circumstance, she worked at blue-collar jobs, raised a family, had a world of friends, and in her spare time was an active leader in a number of charities. My brother, sister and I laugh today at some of her talents and some of her quirks. She was able to put her chin on a child's forehead and tell exactly the child's temperature. She was a consummate hostess: as a youngster, I was often given money to go to the bakery and bring back "nice rolls" before company arrived at our home. For my mom, making people happy was her ultimate life goal. My mother and father also created an environment in our home that enabled me to consider the questions of life and death.

I was born in Yonkers and at age three moved to Farmingdale, a middle class community. I lived with my brother eight years older than me and my sister six years older on Long Island. In comparison to many people, my childhood could best be described as pretty normal. Growing up, life was the local public schools, the backyard catch with my brother and a lot of TV. As a young boy growing up, I was fascinated by history. Not very different from other children born in the 1950s, the television was often my place for discovery. At a very young age, I would watch the original *Biography,* hosted by Mike Wallace. If my recollection is correct, I watched it in the morning when I was home sick from school. This was a frequent occurrence for an asthmatic. It seems as though, each October, as I was growing up, I would get a chest cold which would turn into a serious case of asthmatic bronchitis. As both my parents had to go to work and my older brother and sister went to school, I would stay home with the television as my companion. One morning, I began watching the "Biography of Adolf Hitler." In the show, scenes of dead bodies from concentration camps were shown. At that time, my intellect for rational understanding was ahead of my emotional development and nothing in my mind would explain why human beings would do that to other human beings—and as a young child and into manhood, I needed to know why God allowed evil to exist and what its purpose was here on Earth.

Growing up, few who knew me would have predicted that I would become a high school principal. I certainly was never much of a student and absolutely never took my education very seriously. However, even during those early days when I was a mediocre student, I have been on a search for answers about life's key questions. In my role as a school leader, I attended many funerals for the loved ones of my students and teachers. Unfortunately, on occasions the funeral was for a student or a teacher. Watching the pain so many of us endure has furthered my quest for answers to life and death and its purpose.

The remarkable thing about the way we perceive our existence is that it is not only death that we have misconceptions about, it is that we are truly confused about the purpose of our life. The fact is, few of us understand why we were born onto this planet and the role we have in designing our own life experience. Seldom do we consider that the people we encounter during our lifetime—the people who make us happy and unhappy—and the people who play an integral part in our ability to learn our life lessons, are *not* here as a result of happenstance. What if these individuals are in our lives as a result of our karmic destiny, that being, helping our soul learn the lessons it came to Earth to master? For many, the concept that we choose lessons for our soul to learn prior to our birth is a concept that has never been considered. Even fewer of us give thought to the concept that we may center our life lessons on working out relationships with souls we have encountered in past lives.

The Secrets of Life and Death will reveal that we do not have to succumb to our fears, we can live our lives with love and each day can be filled with joy and meaning. The key to having this better life is based on a greater understanding. An understanding of secrets that many of us had though hidden from us during our lifetime on Earth.

My hope is that the answers offered in *The Secrets of Life and Death* will help you achieve a greater sense of peace, meaningfulness, and joy during your stay on Earth.

Best wishes,
Richard

Part I

Dealing with the End of Life, and Proof That Death Does Not Really Exist

Understanding the Secrets of Death

When we build a house we need a strong foundation or else the house will never be right. When we are building our lives we also need a strong foundation or else our lives will never be right. A house's foundation is built on tangible and physical items such as concrete. Our life's foundation is also based on tangible items; however, these items are beliefs. They are beliefs we hold of how things are and how the universe operates. If our foundation beliefs are solid, we can better deal with life's storms. The problem for so many people is their foundation beliefs are based on incorrect notions. These notions include concepts such as "life ends with death" or "we will face an angry God on Judgment Day" or "life has no rhyme nor reason." A misaligned foundation will always lead to an unstable situation, whether we are talking about a house or a life.

Death is not an end, it is a transition. We have all witnessed what happens when we heat a piece of ice; it quickly transforms into a puddle of water. If we continue to heat the puddle of water, it will make the transition into vapor. Each of these transitions is based on vibration. Heating ice causes the molecules to vibrate faster and the ice transitions to water. Continuing to heat the water causes the molecules to vibrate even faster, and the water transitions to a gas. The laws of the universe are consistent, and so transitions that happen to H_2O when molecules vibrate faster or slower are true of all things—including our soul. We do not die, we transition. When we transition, our soul leaves our body and vibrates faster. As a result, we enter a new world, a world of spirit.

We have incorrectly lived with a foundation belief that we are physical beings with a spiritual side known as the soul. The truth is we are spiritual beings who have slowed down our vibrational pattern so that we can have a physical experience. This slowing of the vibrational pattern is reversed when it is time for us to return back to our spiritual home. Our bodies are no more who we are than the abandoned casing of a cocoon is to a butterfly that has transitioned from its life as a caterpillar.

We never die, welcome to the Secrets of Death.

1. We Never Die

Secret:
There Is Communication with the Other Side

As I was growing up, I had a fear that after I died, I wouldn't know who won the World Series. OK, that was when I was a kid, but as I got older, the fear of death took on a different form. New concerns arose. What about being with my loved ones? What about my own existence?

But there was one question I needed to have answered most: What happens to us when we die? What I have discovered is that there are answers to this question, and they are given to us throughout our lives. If we seek proof, we will find there is more proof than anyone has the time to write about during one lifetime. This is how I came to discover the truth.

In the fall of 1995, my close friends Ivan and Helene were approaching retirement and were looking to move away from the New York area to build their dream house in North Carolina.

The only problem with Helene's desire was that her mother had passed away several years ago. Helene's father was living in a nursing home in the area and suffering from Alzheimer's disease, as well as a variety of other ailments. Helene wanted to speak with her mother about her father and the implications of her and Ivan's plan of moving to North Carolina. Not one to stay with the conventional approach, Helene had found a local medium and wanted to see him in order to contact her mother. Although as a young person I had several psychic experiences, I joined in the ribbing of Helene over the concept of seeking advice from a dead parent. Regardless of the question that Helene wanted answered, the entire premise of looking for answers from the other world seemed pretty absurd at the time. The medium Helene attempted to get an appointment with, Glen Dove, was extremely busy as most good mediums are. Ivan had retired the year earlier while Helene still was teaching. Given the fact that the medium only had appointments available during Helene's school schedule, Ivan took the appointment with Glen Dove. After the initial round of making fun of Helene, I gave little thought to Ivan's upcoming appointment with Glen Dove and went about my life.

The past two decades have been both magical and tragic for my wife and me. In 1992 we were expecting twin boys, but my wife became critically ill during her pregnancy and had to be rushed to the hospital. The days she was hospitalized are mostly a blur in my memory, but the outcome of that experience will live with us both forever. When my wife was admitted, we were told that if the doctors acted immediately there was good chance she would survive but both boys would die. However, the doctors were reluctant to operate because of risk factors. After several days in which they were unable to induce labor, a caesarian had to be performed. The doctor told me that my wife had come through it fine (although she was far from out of the woods), then said nothing about the babies. When I asked, he apologized for the omission and told me, "One is alive, but he won't be for very long." I went to the neonatal intensive care unit after being advised by a hospital administrator that I may want to pay respects to my boy. I had prepared myself to not get emotionally involved. I had just been through the worst hell I could imagine and was lucky to come out of it with my wife alive. I wasn't going to pin my hopes on a 17-ounce baby who was born fourteen weeks premature, especially because the doctor told me there was no chance of his survival. When I went into the intensive care unit, I was led to the incubator of the sickest little boy in the whole hospital. Wires came out of him from everywhere, his skin looked translucent, and his legs were in the position more of a frog than of a person. His little body was not ready to be born, yet there he was. The baby weighed so little that he did not have enough body mass to compose a rear end; he was legs attached to a back.

Despite all the rationalization I had gone through to protect myself from further pain, when I looked at the baby, I emotionally and physically joined in the fight for his life, he was my son. I took the phone number of the neonatal intensive care unit and taped it into my wallet. I told the nurse, I would be calling the unit for months, because it would take that long before we could take him home. I don't know if the nurse was being kind, supportive, or if she believed in miracles—but she agreed. It became our routine to call the hospital each morning to verify that the baby had survived through the night. We would then go to work and follow that with a journey to the hospital. Four and half months later, after hundreds of ups and downs, we took David home. As the months and years have unfolded, we have enjoyed the miracle of David and thanks to God, he is healthy and wonderful. One doctor commented that the odds of David being alive, healthy and unimpaired were 20 million to one. We asked Ivan and another friend, Sydney, to be godparents. As the years passed and we enjoyed our miracle, we have also dealt with the loss of David's twin brother. In this case, closure or a chance to speak to the child we lost seemed impossible. And so we moved on with our miracle, our loss, and our day-to-day life.

One afternoon Ivan called and said that he had to come over. He reminded me that he had gone to see Glen Dove that morning and told me there was a message for me from the other side. I had forgotten that Ivan was going to the medium, but I thought that any message that Ivan thought was being sent to me would be nothing more than some generality that would apply to half the world's population. When Ivan arrived he brought an audiotape of the session. Intrigued, but definitely cynical, I sat down with him to listen to his session with Glen Dove. The first twenty minutes were fascinating, and it was shocking. The medium told Ivan that his mother and father had come from the other side and were now in the room. The medium proceeded to prove it by providing details and idiosyncrasies of Ivan's parents. Dove gave Ivan an exact description of the circumstances of his mother's death and related numerous other items that would have been impossible for him to know. He told Ivan that his mother knew of his upcoming move to North Carolina and that she wished to give him flowers for the new baby due in the family. During the time that Glen Dove was talking of Ivan's family, the name Steven came up. However, the medium did not know where to place it and quickly moved on to other things. As the reading continued the medium said to Ivan I have a message, "I want to say it is for your brother but it is really a close friend. It's about a premature death." Ivan responded, "My brother's wife died in her twenties from cancer." If the medium was a fake, he would have seized on the information and run with it. Instead he told Ivan this was about the premature death of a baby a few years ago. The medium continued, "The baby wants a man whose name begins with an *r*, either a Richard or a Robert, to know that he is doing well on the other side." Glen Dove had previously mentioned a Steven. That was the name we gave the baby who did not survive, but Ivan did not know that, so he was confused by it. Obviously, my wife and I were shaken and relieved, both happy and sad. How does one explain a message of comfort from the other side?

I pondered that question for a while and finally sought out a friend who is very religious. Fully expecting him to reject the story and offer a warning that God frowns upon such things, he said quite simply, "Take it as a gift from God." And we did. I toyed with the idea of going to see the medium myself, but quite frankly I didn't want to be selfish. I had already received more than anyone could expect from such an experience. I had received a message from a son in heaven, on the other side of this worldly existence, without seeking it. Indeed what a gift of peace to know that he is doing well and obviously being watched over. Months passed, and others I knew went to see Glen Dove. Helene, who had started the whole business, finally did go see Glen. Sure enough, Helene's mother did speak with her through Glen and told Helene directly that she should go about her life. Her mother told Helene that her father would soon be joining those on the other side and all would be well. I continued to be amazed as I listened to these audiotapes of a medium who legitimately communicated with those on the other side.

David's godmother Sydney also went to see the medium following Helene and received a few surprises. A man who died in World

War II visited her during the session and told her something that she already knew. The visitor from the other side was also named Sydney, and he told Glen Dove that he is the person she was named after. Sydney had expected to hear from the grandmother she felt very close to in life, however it was her other grandmother who she did not know very well who came forward to speak with her.

Little did Sydney know that she had been chosen, as was Ivan, to be a courier to deliver a message to me. It was during this reading that the second message from our son on the other side was about to be communicated to Sydney. In the course of Sydney's reading, her grandmother, speaking through Glen Dove, directed him to say the following: "Sydney your grandmother is telling me not to try and interpret; they will know what this is all about. The baby wants Richard to know that he is doing well on the other side." Again we were able to hear the message directly as the session was recorded on tape. The second time my son reached out to me, I came away with a different feeling than I had the first time. Although, once again I was shocked to receive a message from the other side, upon hearing it, I was less at peace. I began to wonder if the baby wanted to talk to me directly. I wondered if the decision I had made not to go to the medium was the correct one. I did some soul searching to decide if I should also seek out a channel to Steven through the medium Glen Dove.

In the summer of 1996, I decided to make an appointment. My spirits at this time were running high and low. David was now four years old and doing great. He was a joy to be with. Steven's messages from the other side helped me to deal with his death and the circumstances of losing a child. Under circumstances like these, you are not sure what life has in store for you. A tragedy and a miracle intertwined are hard to understand. However, David's good health was a blessing and we knew it.

In another area of life, my career was not bringing a great deal of joy into my life. I had served for one year as a principal for a superintendent who was insecure and jealous. I barely escaped with my career. As with many fields, in education your reputation is of paramount importance in getting the next job. I was asked back to my former district in a low-level administrative position, as I hoped that a better opportunity would come my way. But as the year passed, new offers did not materialize. As I made an appointment to see Glen Dove, specifically to talk with Steven, I was relaxed having had some time off in the summer, but I was also restless, as my career was not going the way I wanted it to go.

It was a pretty day in August when I went to Glen's Baldwin, Long Island, home office. Despite having heard the tapes of three readings he did for my friends, I was still skeptical that anything would happen when I walked in. This was especially true because Glen did not look the way I had pictured him. In my mind I had envisioned an older man with thick white hair and a white beard. I was expecting a sort of Charlton Heston look when he played Moses coming down from Mt. Sinai with the Ten Commandments. What I found was a typical father in his late thirties. Glen was a former musician who learned that he had a talent as a medium and that people needed his help and would seek him out. As I sat down with him, he started to recap my recent life in precise detail. I was startled by his ability to know what he couldn't possibly know. He informed me that two individuals were standing on either side of me, one much older than the other. He said the older one was named Harry and that he was my grandfather; the younger was named Steven. Although I had heard remarkable things from the taped sessions Glen had done for friends of mine, when I sat down and heard information that absolutely could not be known from ordinary and reasonable means, I was shocked. One of the many speculations people have regarding psychics and mediums is that they do research and that is how they are able to communicate the things that you are told. Or else, they pose leading questions and you provide the information. The hour with Glen was very reasonably priced, and given the cost it would not have been economically worth his time to investigate my background for such information. Additionally, as with my friends, I was told things by the medium that research would not have reasonably revealed. I was also careful not to provide information; I came there to receive information. At one point in the hour, Glen told me that he saw Steven all over me. I believe Steven hugged me in that moment and was attempting to relieve my pain over his loss. I again received a gift that money cannot buy. I am eternally grateful for the opportunity to have encountered a lost son, even in a very unusual way. The message was clear to me as to why Steven sent me messages through others. He was all right on the other side, and he knew that I wasn't all right on this side. I would not give up the fight for him even after he was gone. He came forward so that I could live out my days in peace and accept that his soul had to go to where it was destined to go. We would go about our lives on either side of the divide. One day we will be reunited more fully, but today I am at peace with his existence in heaven. I thank God for the opportunity to know comfort in this way.

Secret:
They Are Watching with Love

Prior to my experiences with Glen Dove, when it came to mediums, I was more than a cynic. I absolutely did not believe we could have an intelligent, discernible conversation with loved ones on the other side. I thought mediums were characters that you would find in a good movie such as *Ghost*. Several friends of mine have gone to see Glen Dove or Tara, the other medium I have seen. My good friend Joe made an appointment to have a reading with Glen several years after his mother's death, though he was pretty cynical about the process. Following his visit to Glen I called him to see how it went. Joe still sounded cynical when he said, "I really don't know about this stuff." I was surprised. This was an unusual response considering the reaction I was used to hearing from friends who had been to see Glen. The usual reaction is shock and amazement. What I was about to find out was that Joe's way of reacting shocked and amazed was to say "I really don't know."

I went over to see Joe and his wife, Katy, and listen to the tape of his session. When I entered the house I immediately heard a different version of events from Katy. She openly expressed her shock and amazement, and she was shaking her head at Joe's reaction. The three of us sat down in the kitchen to listen to the tape. As the reading began someone named Donna came forward through Glen Dove and stated that she had died abruptly from a blow to the head. She said she had trouble accepting her fate but had come to understand why things had to be the way they were. Joe listened to these comments and said nothing. I stopped the tape and asked Joe, "Do you know a Donna?" He replied, "I had a niece named Donna." Then I inquired what had happened to her and Joe replied she was murdered. She was shot in the head and it was a fairly famous case, he said. Her husband, who was a fairly well known figure, killed her. We put the tape back on and listened as Donna sent a message to a woman whose name began with the letters LOR I asked Joe, "Do you know someone whose name begins with the letters LOR?" Joe replied, "I have a sister named Lorie." It was like pulling teeth. Joe wasn't offering any elaborations on his answers. I followed up with, "Is Lorie Donna's mother?" Yes, she was. The reading continued with Donna sending her love from the other side to not only her mother Lorie but to a man named Moe. I asked, "Who is Moe?" though I already thought I had a pretty good guess as to who Moe was. Joe replied, "Moe is Donna's father." Donna told Glen that Lorie and Moe are no longer together, a fact that Joe confirmed.

At this point, I said to Joe, "You have *got* to be kidding me. You are questioning the reading after receiving a message from a niece lost to an act of violence who described the circumstances of her death and her reaction to passing over? Additionally, she stated the name of her parents and told us that they were divorced. You are still not sure that you have spoken with the other side?"

Joe finally admitted that he could not explain the session in any way other than he had communicated with the other side. However, the reading did not end there. As the tape continued to play Joe's mother came forward and talked about Joe's three children. Joe's mother described the exact circumstances surrounding each of his three children. Through Glen Dove she said that Joe's oldest daughter was doing great as she was going to be completing her doctorate. This was true. The grandmother from the other side stated that Joe's youngest daughter was doing fine.

At one point on the tape, Glen Dove related the following message from Joe's mother: "Not that I'm playing favorites, but Joey (Joe's son) needs a little more attention from me this year." Katy was the most shocked at this. It was one of her mother-in-law's favorite phrases: She had a habit of repeating this phrase whenever she was doing something for one of her grandchildren, "Not that I'm playing favorites ..." Then she would go on to state what she was doing for the grandchild. Katy found it incredible to hear a medium attribute that phrase to her mother-in-law several years after the woman had passed away.

It goes without saying that interaction with loved ones who have passed over to the other side is an incredible concept to consider. But the fact that Joe's mother on the other side expressed that she has some ability to affect her grandson's life, in events yet to come on Earth, is truly incredible.

Secret:
When Presented with Evidence of
Communication with the Other Side, We
Frequently Have to Deal with Internal Conflict

We have been socialized in our Western culture to think of death as a passage to a heaven or hell in which a bridge of communication to this world is not possible. We often laugh at, or even pity, those who go to mediums, psychics, fortune-tellers, and others who practice communication with the other side. I know I have always been fascinated by the unexplained, but I had really never believed you could find a medium who could communicate with the other side in a way that is virtually beyond reasonable doubt.

Most people live their lives believing it is impossible for loved ones who have died to contact us. There are others who believe it is possible and suspect that they have been contacted, but still, they aren't quite sure. Many just decide that they can't differentiate between what is real and imagined.

There was a time in my life that I would not have believed a loved one who had passed away could contact me from the other side. Furthermore, the thought that a loved one who had died a whole three decades earlier could coach me on the choices I was about to make in my career was something that I would have considered absolutely absurd. More importantly, I never considered that I could be contacted from the other side in a way that my rational, reasonable mind just could not refute. But quite simply, I was entirely wrong. We can contact loved ones on the other side, and they can contact us.

The fact is we view life through our paradigms. These are filters that are created for us by society, our family, our upbringing, and our own rationalizations about life. Until we remove these filters, we will only see what our filters allow us to see. Why do so many people dismiss proof of life after death? The answer is we dismiss evidence of the other side because we see our own existence through a filter that does not easily allow acceptance of such things.

I can say with certainty that once a person receives an irrefutable message from the other side, life is never the same again. An after-death contact changes the perspective that we have about life and death. The question we have about the immortality of the soul is answered and our natural fear of death is replaced with a fear of the loss of contact with those we love. For those who have had a definitive experience of contact with the other side, there is proof of life after death, and just as importantly, there is proof that God considers our choices during this lifetime. In other words, if there is an afterlife that is proven to exist, then the choices made during this lifetime take on new meaning.

Of course, our thoughts of death and the afterlife are present during our life on Earth. However, given our behavior on Earth, it would be hard to tell that people really consider a life review following death as a reality. It is obvious that the events of life take us on our own road that leads us to think mostly of our immediate concerns. During our lifetime, we are consumed with love and loss, joy and pain. We see selfless heroes and selfish purposely hurtful people. Necessity often makes us more concerned with our job than with our purpose on Earth and the life review we will eventually go through.

Regardless of how we have been socialized throughout our lives, the reality of the secrets of life and death are there for us to consider. Whether we find it easy or difficult to consider life and death in new terms, the more information we are exposed to, the more difficult it becomes to hold on to false notions of existence that we have been brought up with. Internally we are likely to struggle with concepts of the universe that are starkly different than the perceptions we learned as children. However, if we are open minded, a new world of understanding is available.

Secret:
Everything Changes Once We Believe We Never Die

Our entire perspective on life can no longer remain the same when we understand that life is a continuum. Based on our perspective of death, we live on Earth with thoughts and actions that are dominated by our physical needs. We acquire wealth, live in a material frame of mind and acquire false values of what is real and what is not. We are often not kind when it would be easy to be kind.

The main "Secret of Death" is that we do not die. Death is a misnomer for the actual event—we transition from a state of life on Earth to another form of existence in a world beyond Earth. However, existence is still existence—we think, feel, and understand both before and after the transition that we call death. As such, the thought that we can hide our actions during this lifetime, or that acts of unkindness do not matter if you get away with them is a falsehood. Everything we do matters, and once we realize that, we can understand life as an eternal state.

False paradigms permeate our society and our life. Many are centered on the concept that there is only this life (the one on Earth). We say things such as, "You only have one life," to justify doing things. Sometimes those are good things, such as having wonderful adventures. But sometimes we justify bad things, such as taking advantage of others for our own betterment. A more accurate statement about life is, "This life has eternal meaning."

There is a wonderful test to see how the concept of eternal life changes how we approach each day. Tomorrow, wake up and realize that everything you do today is recorded and you will have to review it one day with spiritual beings. Go through the entire day and think of each interaction with other people as reviewable. As a result, do you treat the girl at Starbucks differently? Do you talk more respectfully to people you are angry with? Are you more patient with your children? Ultimately, how many changes do you make in the first twenty-four hours? Try it for one twenty-four-hour period and consider that not only does everything change when we know life is eternal—it changes for the better.

2. The Process of Leaving Earth and Judgment Day

Secret:
There Is Evidence That Death Is a Doorway Back to Another Life

When it comes to communicating with souls that have passed on, we are conditioned to disbelieve any evidence of the afterlife. Many people throughout history have reported out-of-body experiences, frequently describing a common scenario of being drawn toward a light. In these reported cases, individuals have been directed back to their bodies because their time on Earth had not yet been completed. Out-of-body experiences are well documented but often disbelieved by the public. The lifework of Dr. Raymond Moody was to document the stories of those who were dead but somehow had returned to life. In Moody's book, *Life after Life*, these individuals consistently report that life continues after death. Moody is a psychiatrist who interviewed over two thousand people who were dead and returned to life. Most had similar stories, experiences of going into a tunnel toward a light and being received with love and total acceptance. But each returned as they were informed that their life mission was still incomplete. Most of the people who died and returned to life were able to report on their out-of-body experiences and provide information that could validate an experience of leaving one's body.

The front cover of the August 2003 issue of *Reader's Digest* trumpeted, "New Evidence: Life after Death." The article, written by Anita Bartholomew, gave some fascinating information on the subject, while dealing with the afterlife and concepts of the human soul. It begins by telling the story of Pam Reynolds, whose 1991 brain surgery made it necessary for her neurosurgeon, Robert

Spetzler of Phoenix, to stop Pam's heart and her brain function for over an hour while they operated. There is a question as to whether Pam Reynolds was clinically dead for that time period and the extent, if any, of effective brain activity. As with many people before Pam, she later reported that she had an out-of-body experience. She was able to watch her own surgery, and later report on intricate details of the procedure. As the blood was drained from her body, she found herself traveling through a tunnel to a light. At the other end of the tunnel was her long-dead grandmother, relatives, and friends, all of whom greeted her. After a period of time, her uncle led her back to her body. We have been trained to disbelieve or simply find more rational explanations for experiences of the afterlife. However, Pam's description of going into the tunnel and to the light and feeling wonderful during the experience has been documented thousands of times around the world by those who have had near-death experiences. It is amazing that we want to believe that there is life after death and we also have significant evidence, yet still many remain cynical.

HBO produced a special about a study conducted at the University of Arizona that tested a group of mediums, including some world-renowned names, such as George Anderson. All the mediums passed the tests of their abilities with flying colors. Details of the study were published in the book *The Afterlife Experiments*. The author, Dr. Gary Schwartz describes setting up a series of experiments with scientific controls to test whether mediums could in fact communicate with souls on the other side. The study followed strict protocols for evaluating evidence and testing subjects. The mediums were subjected to a series of experiments and did not know the person about to be brought before them (researchers chose the subjects to bring to the medium right before the tests). The evidence gathered indicated that the mediums could actually communicate with the other side. For example, in one reading, the medium communicated with the sitter, and had to return information about the sitter based on asking just five questions. The medium then generated 120 pieces of information with an accuracy rate of 80 percent. There were variances in performance among the mediums, but in general, the results of this study offer significant scientific evidence to complement the deluge of anecdotal stories that make their way around in society. The author's own conclusion from the study is that "information was consistently retrieved that can best be explained as coming from living souls…information sometimes comes that the sitter disagrees with but that turns out to be correct. Also mediums are sometimes corrected by deceased people."

Simply put, with controls established based on scientific protocols, the tested mediums proved that they can contact the other side and bring messages into this world. In the University of Arizona experiments, mediums such as John Edwards and George Anderson were clearly able to bring forward information that cannot be explained by science but can be explained by faith. The researcher, Gary Schwartz, is a pretty convincing skeptic when he says that he is not advocating the survival of consciousness but rather calling for more research on the subject. However, he also says, "the experiments…have brought forth some remarkable events— so many in fact, that to dismiss them is to commit the ultimate scientific sin. When a researcher is fortunate enough to repeatedly witness and collect extraordinary data in many experiments over many years, she or he has the responsibility to respect the reality of those facts."

Many scientists and rational human beings will gladly tell you how ridiculous it is to think we can communicate with the dead. These individuals will ask for proof when in fact no proof would be sufficient to satisfy them. It is important to note that people who will not accept the truth about the continuum of life play an important role to the exploration of life after death. They motivate us to continue to seek more answers and research the questions we have about life and death.

But for the scientist who needs proof of the afterlife, I would like to point out that they themselves haven't answered the most rudimentary question about life, that being, "What is the life force and what does it derive from?" We know that brain waves and heartbeats are indicative of life, but they are not the life force. The truth is that the life force can't be measured, easily described, or identified in terms of where it comes from or where it goes; that is, unless you accept God as the creator, and scientists can't measure God. Scientists measure the artifacts of the life force by detecting the action of the heart and brain, but they can no more clearly identify the life force in the body than they can identify what happens to the life force when it leaves the body. True scientists ask questions even if they know those questions can't be answered. And they also know that if something can't be explained, it does not mean that it does not exist.

Secret:
Finding Our Way Back To Heaven

In the moment in which our heart stops beating and our brain waves are no longer measurable, medical doctors declare that we have died. In fact, we have begun our transition back to our home on the other side of existence, something we now know due to the testimonies of many individuals who have died and returned to life. There are thousands of reported cases of these individuals, providing us with a very significant sample to ascertain what we will all experience at our transition.

At the time of our passing we find ourselves floating outside our body. Sometimes we see spirit guides, but frequently we do not. The first sensation is that have no pain and this is most noticeable in people who were in great pain or discomfort at their time of passing. The ill feelings are all gone. When we view our body, we often have a different perception of it from the outside looking in (for example, one person reported that he thought he was better looking, though, he had just been hit by lightning through a telephone line). Frequently, we want to engage in the conversations we hear in the physical world, but people cannot hear us. We are able to move about and explore the hospital or our immediate surroundings during our time of passing. We also may wish to visit others, especially loved ones. We quickly discover that when we think of them, we are transported without effort to their location.

When we are ready to go on to the next stage of our existence, a tunnel appears and we are drawn to it. As we enter the tunnel, we are drawn to a beautiful, white light. Although the light is incredibly bright, we have no problem looking right at it. The light is in fact the entity that will receive us on the other side. The light does not identify itself and many of those who have passed over and returned have made assumptions of who or what the entity of light is, but exact knowledge seems elusive. It may be God, or an Angel, we simply do not know. For a number of reasons, I believe it is a special Angel designated by God for this exact purpose.

With the "Entity of Light" there are many of your loved ones, friends, and family who have come to greet you with love and total acceptance. It appears that you are in a sort of waiting room as there appears to be a divide that our loved ones can cross to come see us, but we cannot cross at this time. The "Entity of Light" asks us if we are ready to stay on this side. By all accounts, people want to stay because they feel spectacular. However, a few choose to go back because their work on Earth was not done. One of Dr. Moody's interviews involved a man who reported to the "Entity of Light" that he would love to stay but he and his wife have just taken in their troubled nephew. The man believed that if he did not go back, his wife and nephew would not make it successfully. The Light allowed him to go back and told him that when his nephew had grown, the man would come back to the other side. Many of those who Dr. Moody interviewed were told to go back by a loved one from the other side, or the "Entity of Light", because their life on Earth still needed more work.

Following our greetings and reunions with our loved ones who have passed over, the "Entity of Light" leads us on a life review. We see every moment of our lives in a panoramic view that allows us to take it all in. Time isn't a factor; we just simply are able to absorb it all without problem. We not only see all the events of our lives, we feel the joy and pain we caused to the individuals and those who love them. For the souls who have done wonderful things during their lifetime, the life review is joyful. For the souls who have done much harm, the life review is quite painful.

The "Entity of Light" asks us "what do you want to tell me about what you learned?" We are also asked about what we did for other and the "Entity" is quick to point out the difference when we think we did something for others, but we really did it for ourselves. The souls that have gone through this review and subsequently were told to return to Earth report that the incredible thing is that the important moments of our lives are not what we think they are. They are not the great job promotion or the honor we may have won. The great moments are the acts of simple, unselfish kindness that we have done. When the review is over, and if we have been designated to stay, we cross the divide with our loved ones to return to the familiar life in spirit on the other side.

One note: There does appear to be a form of hospital on the other side for souls who have returned in pain to the other side. The stay in the "hospital" helps the soul heal from the difficult life experience and transition back home. However, it appears that the overwhelming majority of souls return healthy and well enough to move back to their life on the other side without difficulty.

Secret:
We Are Forgiven for Mistakes We
Make During This Lifetime

The conventional image of a "Judgment Day" is one in which the soul stands passively before God to find out if they are to be allowed entry to the Kingdom of Heaven or are to be condemned to Hell. But research on the subject has shown a very different event entirely. Instead of a "Judgment Day," what we encounter upon passing over to the other side is a life review, a reflexive look at our life in which we go over the choices we made on Earth during this lifetime and review what it tells God about the maturation of our soul. How much of our life was centered on good deeds? How much of our life was spent in self-absorbed actions, and how much of our life was involved with being the source of intolerance or cruelty?

One of the great questions that arise when contemplating heaven is whether or not people who do bad things on Earth get punished. The answer appears to be a qualified yes and a qualified no. We must remember that God is infinitely capable of forgiveness, and this is a lesson that our soul struggles to master and embody. Each of us makes many mistakes during our lifetime. This is part of the progression of the soul and is an understandable part of our existence as our soul matures. When we pass over to the other side we conduct a life review in which we consider our actions and the choices we made during this lifetime. It is important to remember that this is not like a "judgment day" in which we win or lose. It is in fact, a learning experience. You are the one who is expected to be the judge, along with God. You can't fool God and you can't fool your soul. The soul's life review will take into account the actions you take during your lifetime, and the soul will have to deal with both the good and the bad it evidenced on Earth.

Many human beings want those who have done grave harm on Earth to suffer in the afterlife. Well, they do, in a manner of speaking: They stand before God, and in the life review they must deal with their actions while on Earth. If you have done grave harm that's a pretty terrible punishment! But God is all merciful and understanding and forgiving. One of the reasons our soul chooses to come to Earth is to learn to develop the compassion that is God. God forgives the soul and the soul moves on with its life experience integrated within itself.

Part of our learning on this side is to learn to forgive ourselves as well as others. We make mistakes, and they are a part of our life. It is a law of the universe that tells us God forgives us, and with this knowledge, we have to learn to forgive ourselves. The toughest part of our life review is the ability to forgive ourselves for some of the things we have done on Earth.

However, we do have to learn *why* the actions we took regarding others were wrong. For every action we take on Earth, there is an equal and opposite reaction. When we do good things and live in love, there is more love and good things to come. When we do bad things, we must learn why it was wrong. We have created "karmic debt."Sometimes the learning comes from experiencing the wrong we have done from a new vantage point. But we must remember, we are not punished, even when we are experiencing the pushback from the universe for bad things we have done. We are simply receiving a lesson that was necessitated by the very fact that we had it in us to hurt others. This action indicated that our soul needed a lesson in that area that only experience could provide. Therefore, karmic debt manifested in a future lifetime is not a punishment earned, it is a lesson that must be learned.

Secret:
Souls That Do Not Leave Earth

In 1976 I shared a house with my friend Tim in Rocky Point, Long Island. It was a fairly new house probably around ten years old, built on a hill, somewhat isolated in the woods. Certainly it didn't fit the bill of a haunted house, and I certainly did not expect to have any unusual experiences while living there. One evening when I was home alone watching television, the door slammed. I thought it was my friend, who I shared the house with. The front door opened into an entryway that had a few steps leading up to a second door that opened into the hall opposite the kitchen and next to the living room where I was sitting. When no one came in the door, I got up, opened the door, and looked around. There was no one, and I just figured I was imagining things.

About fifteen minutes later the door slammed again. I was sure it was the front door. After my last experience, I jumped up and went to check out the situation, and again, no one was to be found. At this point, I was sure it was one of my buddies trying to scare me, taking advantage of the fact that my friend and I never locked the front door—we were after all, macho twenty-three-year-olds. I went outside and walked in the dark around the house, sure that I would catch one of my friends. I remember laughing to myself that if this were a horror movie, the music would be going wild about this time. I found nothing and returned to the house. This time I locked the door. Sure enough, even with the door locked, shortly afterward the door slammed again. I then got a baseball bat and sat there with it on my lap, not quite sure what I was dealing with. About an hour later, the doorbell rang. It was Tim. He asked why the door was locked. As I let him in, I said, "You are not going to believe this." As we turned to go into the living room, he asked if the door was slamming. When I asked him how he knew, he said that it had happened to him a couple of days ago when he was home alone. I asked him why he never said anything at the time, and he replied that he didn't think anyone would believe him.

Several weeks later, Tim and I were sitting in the living room watching TV and talking. From where Tim was sitting, you could see into the kitchen. All of a sudden we heard something, and when we investigated, we found the water faucet had been turned on full blast, clearly turned on by something. In fact, it took multiple turns of the faucet to get the water to shut off.

Other unexplainable events kept happening. Charcoal-looking lines would just appear on Tim's hands. He would rub his hands and the lines would disappear. Then without touching anything, the lines would reappear. This phenomenon continued throughout the year we lived in the house, and it stopped when we moved.

In 1978 I visited my future wife in college and met a young lady who lived in her dorm. She said that she was from Rocky Point. I told her that I rented a house there for one year. When I told her about the house, she said she babysat in that same house for a family that had rented it after we left. I asked her if anything strange happened when she was babysitting and she replied, "Yeah, the door would slam, and there was no one there." At a later time, we did find out that someone had died in the house. Someone apparently who still had some tricks up their sleeve.

Ghosts appear to be souls who fail to move on to the other side and seem to be caught in between worlds. For whatever reason, their soul has not been released from earthly existence yet, or they simply do not realize that they should pass over. Another possibility is that the souls know they have passed over and they are coming back to have some fun with us or to resolve issues from their lifetime. In any case, there are spirits on Earth that we would describe as ghosts, and they are able to use energy to do strange things like slam doors and turn on water faucets.

Secret:
God Has Granted Us a Peek at Life on the Other Side

Through messages we have received via mediums and psychics we can certainly get a glimpse into life after death. In a book about the afterlife, *Beyond Death: Conditions in the Afterlife,* the psychic and medium Phillip Solomon and his colleague Hans Holzer attempted to interview people on the other side. Their quest was to find out what that world is like. The idea was to summon spirits of people who had passed away and interview them about their experience on the other side. Solomon reports that people on the other side consistently told him the same thing about the structure of Heaven—that there are seven levels and our souls are to progress from one level to the next to get closer to God.

According to these reports from souls that Solomon contacted, the vast majority of human beings upon passing over return to their existence on the other side on level 2. On level 2, though we are in spirit form, we are able to have the material items our heart desires. There, we are able to meet with loved ones who have passed over and we can spend time as we please. Although information gathered from mediums has presented evidence that we have jobs on the other side to help the universe in meaningful ways. As we progress through level 2, we end up wanting fewer and fewer of the material things that made us happy on Earth. As we learn to leave behind the material desires of our earthly existence, we move toward the spiritual for fulfillment. While on level 2 our soul has to make decisions about its own evolution. Our soul may return back to Earth for more learning or progress upward into level 3. Progressing from levels 3 through 7 get us closer and closer to God. It appears that even those on the other side still living at level 2 know little of existence at these higher levels. Souls that have committed terrible acts on Earth have much to learn and as such, do not progress to level 2. These souls are sent to level 1, an existence of debauchery with separation from God (until they learn this type of existence is meaningless). When they have learned the wrongfulness of their acts, they can work on having their soul progress.

The interesting thing about this account of heaven we have from Solomon is its consistency with the Hebrew view that there are seven levels of heaven and that God resides on level 7.

A simpler approach to explaining the other side comes from George Anderson. He writes in *Walking in the Garden of Souls*, "When we graduate to the hereafter, we learn all about the things that happened to us on the Earth and begin to understand them. The soul, free of hurt and hopelessness, becomes perfect again in the hereafter. We never lose our personalities because that is what makes our soul unique, but we do lose the dysfunction that plagues us sometimes in our existence here. Now you know why they call it 'Heaven'."

Yes there is an afterlife and an entire complex world on the other side. In this world, we exist in a form that vibrates at a greater frequency, devoid of the pain we sometimes experience on Earth. Additionally, there is much room for the soul to continue to grow and progress. There are multiple examples of proof that our loved ones on the other side are aware of what is happening in our lives on Earth and what might happen in our near future here on Earth.

Probably the most common question people have about the other side is whether we are with our loved ones. The answer is you will be together with your loved ones after you pass over. In fact, you will be able to see whomever you wish to see.

We get pieces of the puzzle of what life is like on the other side from culling data from a variety of legitimate mediums and parapsychologists. It is obvious that each person continues to have a role to contribute on the other side from some of the reports we get. For example, Solomon's collaborator, parapsychologist Hans Holzer, reports that his research on the other side indicates that we all have jobs in level 2. He also describes the other side as operating as an efficient "bureaucracy." It is also obvious that our soul continues its growth on the other side. There is much for the soul to experience and not all of that experience seems to be here on Earth.

Recently, I picked up an audiotape of a reading with Glen Dove. I thought the tape was of a reading with me, but in fact it turned out to be a reading with my wife, Benay, in the summer of 2003. I listened and was fascinated as the medium pieced together the story of our son David. He asked my wife, "Who was David? Was there another child on the other side? Were they twins?" Then he told my wife that they are working together, even now. Somehow, David still has help from his brother on the other side. Exactly what kind of help it is and how it comes to him we may not know while we are on this side. But it is fascinating to know that a brother can and will take time out of his life on the other side to help his brother on this side.

Secret:
What Is Hell?

Quite simply, Hell is separation from God. When an entity does terrible things, it separates from God. As such, the universe sends the entity to a different level of existence to learn from its mistakes. However, this level is one that is noted by its separation from God.

On Earth, individuals who are greatly damaged by the life experience frequently repress their *soul energy*. As such, these entities separate from the love that drives all things. Life for these people has been a painful experience, and as a result of their pain, they hurt others around them. They are in a "hell on Earth," and they work to try and create the same condition for others.

The notion that one evil act or deed, or even a series of bad acts, condemns a soul to hell for all time simply is not true. The good thing is that God has created a system in which these souls can reclaim a place in his love. They do it by coming to understand that what they were doing was wrong and learning from experience. The universe does have an accountability system in place and when we pass over to the other side we must go through a life review. During our life review, we feel all the pain we caused and have to deal with the way we conducted our lives. However, placement in hell is not permanent for any soul. God is love, and as the ultimate form of love will accept back souls that have learned their lessons and therefore have paid their karmic debt by understanding the wrongfulness of the acts that placed them in a place separated from God in the first place.

3. Advice from the Other Side

Secret:
Career Advice from the Other Side? Give Me a Break!

Since the summer of 1996, I know a number of people who have gone to Glen Dove or other legitimate mediums. They have left the encounter stunned with the medium's ability to communicate with our loved ones on the other side. There is a variety of interesting aspects to these encounters, not the least of which is *advice*.

My grandfather gave me advice regarding my career when I was at a crossroads regarding what direction to head in. My wife had scheduled a reading with Glen Dove in the spring of 1997, as life would have it, at the exact time I had a job offer that I considered declining. When she went to the appointment she was hoping to hear from the son she had lost and to settle some issues with her father, who had passed over to the other side. My grandfather had told me from the other side in a session during the summer of 1996 to stay calm regarding my career. He told me that someone had told me to sit at a certain desk, and it was the wrong one (which was quite accurate). Furthermore, he stated that in the next year, I would have another tough year as a school administrator, but after that my former title would return to me. In the winter of 1997, I began sending my résumé out to once again become a principal. There was one district I was especially interested in staying away from. Long Beach, on Long Island, had a history of destroying principals—in fact Long Beach High School was known for it. Its reputation was that it had an especially difficult teaching staff and board. However, when you are going for a new job, interviews are important to hone your skills and help prepare you to get the jobs that are desirable. There were two jobs that were very interesting to me; one was at the high school I had graduated from. A number of people had contacted that district on my behalf, and I felt that I had an excellent chance of getting the job. Meanwhile, Long

Beach was moving more quickly with the interview process than the other districts and I was invited in for two interviews. The second interview was with the Board of Education, and it went very well. When you don't really want a job, you tend to interview well because you are relaxed. The morning after the board interview I received a phone call from the assistant superintendent for personnel who told me that the internal candidate was likely to get the job. If he didn't get the high school position he would have been returned to the elementary school as a principal, and he would bump people out of the jobs they had the past year. One of the people that would be bumped was the sister-in-law of a board member. When I heard that, I was pretty certain that I wasn't going to be offered that job. The representative from Long Beach inquired as to what salary I would expect if I was offered the job, once again informing me that this was not a job offer and the internal candidate was probably getting the job. Not wanting the job anyway, but realizing a job offer would not hurt me in the other districts I had applied to, I gave her a salary that was fairly low, and I went about my day not giving it another thought. That night around 11 P.M. the phone rang and it was picked up by the answering machine. It was the assistant superintendent from Long Beach, and she was calling my name out through the answering machine to pick up the phone. I sat up in bed confused as to why she would be calling, and listened to the message. She said, "Richard our board appointed you high school principal tonight." I started to yell at the answer machine, "You can't do that!" My wife told me to calm down and just call tomorrow and decline. I informed my wife that declining the job after appointment is not quite that simple. This type of appointment is done in public session. I told my wife this is not a job offer, it is an appointment. Turning it down will make me look ridiculous since no one appoints someone to a job without offering the job first, except Long Beach, that is. Afraid of political fallout, and unfortunately enamored with my performance at the interview, the board rushed through the appointment. A refusal on my part would result in a fairly substantial article in *Newsday* (Long Island's only major paper) and the subsequent negative publicity that would accompany it. The phone call came on Tuesday night, prior to a several-day break for the April holidays. That year we had a split Easter/Passover vacation, and we were due to have the days off from Thursday through the following Tuesday. The assistant superintendent of Long Beach called me at work on Wednesday morning and directed me to come in and sign the contract. I responded that the interview process is a nice way to meet people in the district, but ultimately I will have to have a strong working relationship with the superintendent and I have not even had a conversation with him. We scheduled a meeting with the superintendent for the following week and this gave me the weekend to think about what to do next. I didn't want the job, but if I turned it down, it was likely to seriously hurt my candidacy in other districts.

My wife had scheduled her appointment with Glen Dove on the Monday of this short vacation. As my wife was having her session, Glen stated, "I know this is your reading, but your husband's grandfather Harry wants to come in and he has a message for him." My wife instructed Glen to let Harry come forward. Harry said to my wife, "Tell Richard to go with the new opportunity, dot the i's and cross the t's." As it turned out, I met with the superintendent and liked him very much. I took my grandfather's advice from the other side; I accepted the job and went with the new opportunity.

But if you told me that I would get career advice from a grandfather who had passed away over three decades ago…I would have responded—"Give me a break!" I would like to say that prior to these experiences I was open-minded. But the truth is, I wasn't. I never believed that we could have advice from a loved one on the other side. I was wrong.

Secret:
Messages from the Other Side May Provide Advice and Comfort, But You Still Have to Live Your Life

I have come to understand that it is not uncommon to receive advice from a loved one on the other side. As I related, I had the experience of my grandfather Harry coming forward in my wife's reading to urge me to change my destiny by taking a job offer. But I also had advice from him on two other occasions.

As I mentioned, the first time I went to have a reading in the summer of 1996, my grandfather spent a great deal of time talking about my career as a school administrator and how life had not been fair to me. He informed me through the medium that the next year was not going to be easy. He said that in fact it would be more difficult than the past year. But he advised me to stay calm and said that my job title would return to me at the end of the year. And that is exactly what happened.

In one of my subsequent sessions with Glen Dove, in 1999, he sent a message to my brother Michael regarding events that were about to unfold. During the reading Glen said a message was coming forward for a Michael. I said Michael was my brother and inquired about the message. Glen told me that the message was from my grandfather Harry. He was advising Michael to stay calm and keep things in perspective. My grandfather used the phrase, "As bad as it is, it will be OK." Shortly after that reading, my nephew unexpectedly developed a blood clot that affected the sight in one of his eyes. It was scary, and my nephew lost a good deal of his sight in that eye, but my brother stayed calm just as my grandfather had advised. And as bad as this experience was, my nephew has moved on with his life.

In a reading I had with the other medium I have seen, Tara, she asked me who Gloria was. I informed her that Gloria was a cousin of mine who passed over. Tara told me that Gloria was watching my mother in Florida sneak in food to eat at home, and

Gloria wanted my mother, a diabetic, to stop it. Sometimes the message we receive from the other side is a heads-up, sometimes just a confirmation of what is. In another session with Tara she asked, "Who is Flo?" I told her my mother's name is Florence and some people call her Flo. Then she asked, "Who calls her 'a tough cookie?'" I laughed as I told Tara that my father calls my mother "a tough cookie." Then I was also told that my mother's foot was swollen. When I later called Florida and spoke to my mother, she confirmed that this was true. The first time I had a reading with Tara, she asked me, "Who is David?" I informed her that he is my son. She asked me if I had a picture of him. When I showed her David's picture, she asked me if there was another child we had with him who had passed over.

Messages from the other side are fairly common, but they don't always tell you what you want to hear. People going to a medium to make a particular contact or to seek information regarding something on this side may be disappointed. It is important to note that those on the other side will tell us certain things and choose to keep other things from us. Sometimes you can go to a legitimate medium and not receive a message from the person you wanted to hear from. My friend Patty lost her daughter Cathy in a rock-climbing accident while Cathy was in college. When she went to Glen Dove, he told her that her daughter had been killed in an accident in which her neck was broken. He told her that she died instantly and without pain and that she was teaching on the other side. To my surprise, Patty was very disappointed by the reading. Instead of coming away with a sense of relief that her daughter Cathy was fine on the other side, she was upset because she wanted assurances from her reading that nothing bad was going to happen to her other children. When the future of her other children was not discussed, she was very disappointed and considered the reading a waste of time.

When a person goes to a legitimate medium, they may still be highly suspicious about the legitimacy of the whole affair. Proof of legitimacy can come in funny ways. Sometimes a body motion can confirm the messenger from the other side. This was the case

with Pam, who went to Glen Dove shortly after her grandmother
Alice died. Pam and Alice were very close, and Alice was very
healthy even though she was in her eighties. She was going about
her daily routine on the sidewalks of the neighborhood in Brook-
lyn where she lived when she was hit by a bike. Alice passed over
and Pam was eager to hear a message from her. Alice did come
forward in Pam's reading and her message to Pam was to stop
fighting with her mother Joan. The fascinating part of this reading
is that when Glen was communicating the message to Pam from
Alice, he put his hands together as if he was praying and moved
them up and down just as Grandma Alice used to do. Additionally, Alice told Pam that she was aware of the things that Pam had
said to her when she was lying in a coma prior to passing over, and
thanked her.

Each time I have gone to a medium, my grandfather Harry
comes forward by name and gives advice or signals that he is who
he says he is. For example, in a reading with Tara, he said to remind my father of a shoeshine kit. I had no idea what he was talking about until I talked to my father. It turns out that during the
Depression, against the wishes of my grandfather, my father would
take a shoeshine kit into the subways and shine shoes to earn money
for Boy Scout outings.

There are of course, many frauds willing to exploit people for
profit. I'm sure there are many who claim to be mediums just waiting to take your money. But there are also gifted people who are
able to let you know that your loved ones are all right. I have encountered two mediums, Glen Dove and Tara, who are genuinely
gifted, and their abilities cannot be explained with rational argu-
ments. However, there are many others. Somehow these specially
gifted individuals have the ability to receive messages from people
on the other side. Thousands have seen James Van Pragh and other legitimate mediums on television. These gifted mediums offer
people who have lost a loved one great relief and allow us to understand that our loved ones do not die, they simply pass over.

I should put in a word of warning here. I do not believe that we should seek advice from the other side. If loved ones want to offer it in a session with a medium, so be it. Life is meant to be lived, and we should trust the little voice inside our head to do the right thing. For all we know, that little voice is already a loved one sending us a message. How are we to know if our intuition really isn't something other than that?

Secret:
Our Loved Ones in Heaven Have a Purpose in Attempting to Communicate With Us

To the surprise of some, souls on the other side make efforts to communicate with their loved ones on this side. They probably do this because they know how much we miss them and the pain their passing has caused. After we experience the loss of a loved one, we hope that they have found comfort in heaven. We wonder what the afterlife is like and what our loved ones' everyday existence is like. Many of us wonder if our loved ones can hear our thoughts and words. Many of us pray for a contact from the other side and wonder if we will all be together again one day. In some cases we live in agony, consumed with the thought that our loved ones' last moments on Earth were filled with fear and pain. Despite the myriad stories about contact with souls on the other side and the teachings of religions that speak of an afterlife, many in our society simply need more proof of an afterlife to find peace.

Although we receive many messages from the other side, receiving a message from a deceased loved one that we can accept as real is difficult. The most common reason for a message coming from the other side is that a loved one who has passed into heaven is attempting to ease our pain on Earth and is helping to guide us. Souls that pass over most commonly attempt communication with the living on Earth through dreams and thoughts. However, many people have noted other signs, such as moved objects, a particular smell, or a song on the radio at a significant moment.

The point is these experiences are common, but you've been trained to not accept any notion that a communication from the other side has occurred. Perhaps you can try to suspend disbelief and open up to the idea that communication might happen. In fact, the more open you are, the more you will realize how frequently it does actually happen.

We often hear about people who have received a message from a loved one who had died. Commonly we dismiss these encounters as hallucinations of people who needed to communicate just one more time with a person he or she loves. The truth is our loved ones on the other side often do communicate with us.

Perhaps the most common encounters come while we are asleep and in a dream state or while we are driving in a car alone. These two situations seem to be most ideal for those on the other side to begin communicating with us because the mind is the most open to contact. Those who doubt that we communicate with the other side need to spend some time reviewing the work of famous mediums such as James Van Pragh, Sylvia Brown, George Anderson, or Jonathan Edwards. But everyone receives messages and has contacts, whether they recognize the communication or not. When we have a thought, who can tell whether something or someone has influenced that thought.

For the living who are considering communicating with those in the afterlife, there is often doubt about whether a message can even get through. But you can always count on it that when you think about your loved ones on the other side, they always receive the message. When thinking of your loved ones, think good thoughts and think of love. They will hear you and appreciate the communication.

Secret:
Some Souls Are More Active After Death Than Others

On September 27, 2008, my mother went home to the other side. During her stay on Earth, she was a special woman who engaged in many civic activities and was the president of numerous charities. However, she did not need or seek the spotlight; she was just happy being a worker bee in the background. She loved people, especially children, and never quite accepted the cruelty and pain that exists in our world. For those close to her, emptiness appeared in their lives when she returned home to the other side. Some souls just have a tremendous influence on those around them.

But my mother's passing was not to be her final say. The day of her funeral, I was making my father breakfast in my kitchen in our Long Island home when the TV set suddenly went on. I was somewhat shocked, knowing my father didn't know how to turn the TV on given the complexity of the remote, cable box, and TV. I turned to him and asked, "Did you just turn the TV on?" He replied, "It is OK," as though he thought that I had turned it on. Apparently neither of us had turned it on. For whatever reason, it appears that souls on the other side have an easier time manipulating electronics than other items in our physical universe. We took it as her final good-bye. However, Mom's personality was not one to fade into the background, and she was just beginning with the ways she would be intervening with us.

My brother encountered a series of incidents that included: one day returning to his car that had been locked securely and finding all the windows open; getting into his elevator and having the button for his floor light up automatically without him touching it; and returning to his car to find the seats moved up and the steering wheel moved into a new position. My father also had a similar occurrence with his car--a car that he had locked up securely and left parked had all the windows open when he returned.

PHOTO FROM MIKE'S PHONE THAT MYSTERIOUSLY APPEARED ON SCOTT'S COMPUTER

But perhaps the two most surprising interactions occurred with my nephew Scott. He was tending to his infant daughter who was in the hospital, and he called on the spirit of his grandma for help in making everything right. At the very moment he reached out to grandma, the lights in the room blinked. Subsequently, his daughter was fine. Even rarer is what occurred with his computer. My brother and sister-in-law had left a rock on Mom's grave with the inscription, "LOVE U." They took a photo of the rock with their cell phone and, on returning to Florida, discussed it with Scott. Scott offered to transfer the photo from the cell phone to his computer and print out a picture. My brother said he was tired and going home, so they would do it another time. They said good-bye and left.

Later on Scott went to his computer and among pictures he had taken of his daughter was the picture from the cell phone, which had somehow been transferred to the computer. The cell phone had never been hooked to the computer. There was also no rational explanation for why the image file of the rock from the grave was placed between other pictures that had previously been saved on the computer. To add to the mystery, the date of transference was different than on all the other photos. The date stamp read 12/31/79. We wondered if this date had some special reference to my mother and called my father to find out. He couldn't think of anything in particular about New Year's Eve 1979 and so the mystery goes on. My brother did not send the photograph to my nephew's phone or computer, but there it was.

My brother was in a great deal of pain following the loss of our mother, and he did not quite have my belief system regarding life after death and the ability of legitimate mediums to make contact. I scheduled separate appointments with Glen Dove for my brother and myself in December 2008. Within minutes of the reading with Glen, my brother was told by Glen that his mother was thanking Nancy for everything she did. Nancy is my brother's daughter who lived around the corner from my mother. Nancy would bring the great-grandchildren over to see my mother and spend time with her. This was a gift that she greatly valued in the last years of her life. An hour later, I went into the reading with Glen, who told me that the motherly presence in the room was Florence or Marian. I told Glen that it was Florence and asked him how he came up with the two names. He said that the presence showed him in his mind two women who were receptionists in an office in the building, their names were Florence and Marian.

My mother has done other things to let us know she is still around. My brother in particular is confused as to why we have been gifted with so much contact while others who lose loved ones have little or no contact. That is one of the secrets that we will still have to work on discovering.

Secret:
Loved Ones on the Other Side Try to Help Our Soul Progress

We frequently receive messages from the other side. These messages are easy to hear, but for many they are hard to accept. The message is for us to forgive, to help those who have hurt us, to respond to evil by contrasting it with goodness. Our human side often rejects those concepts and often doesn't trust the message from the other side that is being delivered through our soul. The soul is connected to the universe, and we need to align our lives with the soul's purpose. There is no punishment for not hearing the soul's message, but a life separated from soul is a life filled with pain. If you want to see happiness, it would be in the faces of Gandhi, Mother Theresa, and others who have aligned with the soul's true mission of doing for others.

The more we hear the message from the other side, the more we understand that soul growth occurs when we do for others. The more we listen intuitively, the more we understand that all the individual souls on Earth are part of one collective entity. Do we receive messages from entities on the other side? The answer is: Every second of every day.

As cited in Sidney Kilpatrick's *Edgar Cayce: An American Prophet*, the great twentieth century psychic Edgar Cayce frequently referred to the fact that our soul has come to Earth with lessons to learn from prior lives. Therefore, the universe has gone so far as to give us instructions on what we are to accomplish during this lifetime. We interact with entities from the other side during our stay on Earth; we come to Earth with a plan that has been developed; we know that at the end of our lesson we will return to the other side; yet we question whether the afterlife is part of our lives. We human beings are an interesting group.

In Summary

The Secrets of Death

Simply stated, we don't die. We leave our earthly body behind, but the physical body we lived in during our earthly existence was never who we truly are. That body is simply a container for the soul. Our soul survives death and thrives on the other side. In many ways, the other side, or what we call heaven, is our real home. We reunite with loved ones on the other side while we still monitor and try to influence our loved ones on Earth.

Once we start looking, we find there is more proof that our soul continues on to the other side than one would reasonably expect. Thus the answer to the question of what happens after death is clear: Death is a transition to the form of life we enjoy on the other side. From all the evidence, life on the other side is wonderful, and there is much to be joyous about when our stay on Earth has been completed.

We also know that individuals called mediums have the ability to communicate with souls on the other side. From these communications we do get a glimpse of what exists in heaven.

It is also true that there is a life review and an accounting of the experiences the soul had during the earthly stay. The concept of punishment on the other side for bad deeds on Earth is probably best described as soul repair. When the soul causes harm on Earth and returns to Heaven, it is likely sick and needs to be repaired in a way that Heaven handles those situations. Nothing we do on Earth exists on its own. Every action is in the context of the larger story of the universe.

All in all, go in peace knowing we don't die, our loved ones don't die, and a happy reunification is in store for all of us with our loved ones on the other side. The Secret of Death is that it is a doorway back home, for we never die—life is eternal.

What Are the Secrets of Life

Wouldn't it be great if life came with a user's manual or a road map to navigate through life? *The Secrets of Life* Part II and Part III are just that. They are a user's manual for navigating and under standing life.

In Part II the manual deals with why we are on Earth in the first place and what are we to do with our time here on Earth.

In Part III the manual deals with how we can live a better life once the secrets have been revealed.

Part II

Why We Are Here and What Does God Want of Us?

1. Life Lessons through Experience

Secret:
The Earth Is a University Built So the Soul Can Study and Learn

Life on Earth is a choice we have all *made.* The soul's purpose in leaving heaven for a life on Earth is to grow in a way that is difficult to experience on the other side. The soul has left heaven, journeyed to a new place to study, and that place is the planet Earth. Earth is a place that God has created for his children to learn and grow. On Earth, the soul can learn lessons on love, fear, accomplishment, contentment, tragedy, loss, enchantment, and on and on. We choose to be born and have these experiences on Earth in order to move forward in our spiritual progression. The purpose of our life on Earth is progression.

The special thing about the soul's course of study on Earth is that each soul takes an independent study program uniquely designed to suit the individual. Although it appears that two individual souls may be having a similar experience, in fact the lessons their souls are experiencing are quite distinct. Even though these souls may come together in the same environment at the same time, they are each likely to be learning different lessons. For example, famous stars are together at a party. These souls may have many things in common and may be learning about the adulation of adoring fans, economic success, and having a talent that separates them from others. But each had a different childhood, different adult relationships, different fears and concerns. Each soul has a customized experiential context in which to learn its lessons.

It is hard to accept the concept that this world may be the area that we are merely passing through and the other side is our true home, but that in fact is the case. We are here to experience emotions and feelings we cannot experience on the other side. Our soul has knowledge of all things, but the soul needs experience to truly understand.

Without coming to this world our soul might understand pain and suffering as a bad thing, but to achieve true understanding of what that means our soul needs direct experience of those emotions; emotional situations that are not possible to have on the other side. We are growing through our experiences and this allows us to be richer and more aware when we return to our true home. God designed earthly existence to give our soul a unique course of study. As when students go away to college, the time is real and hopefully enjoyable, but it is not home. It is a place you go for a time to study.

Our life purpose on Earth is to help the soul develop in a course of varied experiences. While we are on this Earth and dealing with the experience, there are times that we would never believe we chose to have this experience. But the souls on the other side see it differently, and promise us that one day, we will too. They promise that we will appreciate the painful experience as a necessary learning tool for the soul. We may cognitively know that something is wonderful or painful—but we really don't know until we have lived through the experience.

Welcome to the University of the Earth! It comes complete with an athletic program, theater program, and a food plan. It is also toughest in our early years when we lack wisdom and our senior years when we face changes that can be scary. Just as a college experience ends and we have to move on, so does our stay on Earth. We all return home—with new experiences and new-found wisdom.

Secret:
How to Pass the Tests of Life

One of the great questions we have about our lives is whether or not life is a test or a measurement of our worthiness for life in heaven. This question is based on a view of God's universe as one in which life is actually a game in which some win and some lose. Life is a school in which our soul integrates learning through experiences. Accordingly, as we learn lessons through experience we are ultimately here to learn to embrace love and dismiss fear. There are no tests that we can fail that will condemn us for all time. However, life does test us, in order to measure how well we have learned the important lessons of love.

Life is full of adventures. Adventures are exciting because they involve risk and pain. If you so desire, you can think of these difficult moments as tests. If you view life this way, it is fair to say that life has tests for all of us. These tests force us to make choices that set us on a particular course for the rest of our life. What determines the lessons our soul learns is based on the decisions we make when we reach the crossroads of our life. Make one choice and we will have one outcome, make another choice and we will have a different life experience.

In September of 1992, I faced a test between my fear and my love. My son David, born prematurely in July 1992, had reached mid-September and we were hopeful that things were going in the right direction. Our daily routine upon waking each morning was to call the hospital to check on how David's night went. On Friday night, this particular September weekend, I left the hospital around 10 P.M. and David was on 28 percent oxygen and doing pretty well (room air is 21 percent oxygen). Early Saturday morning, I called to check on David's night and I was told that he was in bad shape and was on 90 percent oxygen—David was dying. After all that we had been through, it took every ounce of strength I had in my body to go to the hospital. I wanted to crawl up in the fetal position and lay in a dark corner. Still I found the strength and went to the hospital. When I arrived, I found the doctors had not followed my directive regarding the gathering of information they were seeking. As they were attempting to gather information on the use of steroids with premature babies, they wanted to collect urine from David. I had given the hospital permission to collect the urine as long as David's legs were wrapped because that was the way he was comfortable. When I arrived, I found David's legs unwrapped and he was kicking slowly with whatever energy he had left. When David's legs were unwrapped he would kick and put himself in distress. The hospital utilized so many different nurses and doctors that no one knew the babies' special characteristics. I knew that David would kick and place himself in distress if his legs were free. When I arrived at the hospital, the doctor performing the data gathering had already gone home after making his Saturday morning rounds, while my son remained in grave danger. In charge of the unit was a young doctor serving on a fellowship. I directed him that I was withdrawing my permission to collect the urine and that he was to have the urine collection bag removed and to wrap David's legs. The doctor reluctantly complied. Before our eyes, the monitors indicated David's oxygen saturation moved up immediately and he recovered steadily throughout that long Saturday.

I look back on that day as a test of my courage and will to fight. When I got the bad news that morning I simply wanted to crawl up in a dark corner of my bedroom and be left alone in my fear and despair. Getting dressed and going to the hospital took courage and ultimately led to saving my son's life. Courage isn't the absence of fear; it is doing what you have to do despite the fear. When you face your ultimate fears, get up and fight—you have no other choice. Ultimately, my soul learned the important lesson that love can and will defeat fear. We pass the tests of life when we come from a place of love.

Secret:
Our Experience Teaches Us to Balance Our Wisdom with the Counsel of Others

Our life experience is centered on interacting with others. One of the realities of life is that there are people in your life who want to set your agenda. They also frequently want to set your schedule. The agenda or a time frame for events that another person is trying to impose on you is *their* agenda or time frame. This comes from all walks of life: It might be your next-door neighbor or the people you work with or even your best friend. One indication of a successful marriage is that the two parties come to understand the degree of independence the other party needs. In other words, a married couple comes to allow a balance of individual and mutual needs in their relationship.

The attempt to control another person happens in virtually all relationships and may even involve a subordinate person doing the controlling. For example, when a person finds himself or herself in the position of being a new boss he or she is frequently subjected to an employee's self-anointment as the guide for their new boss. Employees are desirous of the new boss moving forward on their agenda, not the new boss's agenda. This is not because the employees are bad, but because they think they are right, or see a personal advantage in the suggested action, and people want to control their own lives.

In looking at situations in your life, it is important to recognize that you need to set your own agenda and time frame for taking action while still understanding the needs of others. People will want you to solve the problems they want solved, to live your life or pursue your career as they would have you do it. Trust your instincts, and if you have an older and wiser mentor, this is a good time to seek advice.

Another example involves children who have loving but controlling parents. Parents want to make sure that their child makes the right decisions in life and does not get hurt. But life is about discovery and children will need to make their own decisions and their own mistakes, within reason. Teenagers, for the most part, are not ready for independent flight and will need more guidance in making their decisions, but sometimes the parental control extends well into the child's adulthood.

The best way for adult children to deal with controlling parents is to let them know you appreciate and respect their thoughts. But at the same time let them recognize that life is a great adventure, and you need to choose for yourself the road that your journey will proceed on. It is important in this case for the younger generation to consider that their parents have gained wisdom through experience and that their thoughts should not be discounted lightly. For the parent it is important to recognize that their job is not only to give their child roots to grow but also wings to fly.

To a certain degree, we are all trying to control our own lives but sometimes some of us do not see how others are trying to control our lives. It is important to remember that among those others who are trying to control our lives, some are offering the benefit of their wisdom. The mature choices in life are the ones that allow us to take control of our own life, set our own agenda rather than someone else's, but also recognize wise counsel when it is being offered and learn to accept it. The secret of integrating our wisdom with the wisdom of others is to learn to live in balance. Balance is established in life by learning both from our own experiences and from the experiences of others.

Secret:
The Need to Be Important Is Often Harmful to Others

For so many, the life experience is concentrated on becoming important, famous, or wealthy. Many souls have the need to stand out from the crowd. One question that is seldom asked is how important is it to God that we become famous or wealthy during our lifetime? The answer is that those things appear to be pretty insignificant to the creator. But the desire to be important is not a problem in its own right. The problem is when the need to be important is more compelling in a person than the need to be good and decent. The need to feel important can be dangerous and can lead us to shallow behavior. T.S. Eliot said that half the harm in the world is done by people who want to feel important.

There is nothing wrong with wanting to be important if a person goes about it in a non harmful way. If you live your life doing the right thing, you will be important to all the people who it is worth being important too. Be a good father, mother, neighbor, worker, or leader. Just be a good person and the rest will take care of itself. In fact, when you do the right thing in your life, you can't help but be important. *Trying* to be important is always forced, never natural, and leads people to make poor choices and compromise their relationships.

It is important to recognize that the need to be important is based on our *earthly* needs. On the conscious level that the soul resides in, and in God's eyes, we are all important—equally important. And there is no way we can become unimportant to the creator.

Having the status of importance on Earth is something others decide for us. It is not a state that we can choose to be on our own—others make us important. Our life experience is to be lived to learn, and we learn by understanding the importance of others. When we see evidence that others are important to us, we instantly become important to them. So the best advice regarding our normal desire to be important is live your life to help others. You will be important and stand out as a righteous person whose life makes a difference.

2. Soul Growth and Progression

Secret:
God's Plan for Our Life Is Clear

The great question of humankind: why are we here and why did God create Earth and the earthly experience? During those times in life when things do not go our way, we question our life, luck, and the reason we are in this world. For some, difficult times cause confusion regarding our relationship with God. Our confusion about life is based on the fact that we have never really figured out why we are here and what life is really about. At face value, the whole life experience doesn't make a great deal of sense. For many of us, at certain points in our lives, we live in a world that is seemingly devoid of justice, rhyme or reason.

Rational people might respond, how can the many terrible things that we see in our world constitute all that is right? Some people see life's bad occurrences as random and happenstance. Some people consider the terrible things that happen as God's retribution to people who have sinned, and these views are based on the assumption of a reward or punishment system. Still others see life's hardships as a great test that God has created for us.

The truth is life has a justice system, and rhyme and reason for all events. In order to understand our world, try and think about life as an experience that we *chose* to encounter. Consider that in life we have an array of separate moments tied together by a single thread called a *lifetime*. The experiences of that lifetime have a common purpose. Taken in their totality, they help our soul learn and mature. Going one step further, in addition to this lifetime are the lessons of a series of lifetimes strung together and what we end up with is an enlightened soul.

The life experience helps to provide the soul with valuable insights. If you accept that life is an experience that we chose to encounter, wouldn't our curiosity desire the whole experience? Our soul learns through this lifetime the good and the bad, love, rejection, exhilaration and, yes, even the pain. Each experience is a meaningful learning tool for our soul. All our life experiences contribute to the soul's growth.

It does seem crazy to think we come willingly into a stay on Earth aware that very bad things might happen, and probably will happen. It seems even crazier to think that we might have chosen to come here with the express purpose of experiencing some of the worst that life has to offer. But when you look deeper and ask some fundamental questions, the concept becomes clearer. How is your soul to understand deep pain if it doesn't experience it? How is your soul to understand fear and despair without experiencing it?

While it is true that our soul is from God and all-knowing, the soul's knowledge needs clarification and illumination. The soul is consciously aware of pain and joy, but it seems that in God's grand design, true understanding involves experience. We are here on Earth to experience the good, the bad, the mundane, and the whole deal. The things we don't experience in this life, we will experience in other lifetimes. That is why we are here: we are here to illuminate and enlighten our soul through the experience.

We have heard all kinds of variations of why bad things happen to people. But what if the explanation for why bad things happen to people is so plainly simple? What if everything that happens to us during our lifetime has purpose? What if everything that we experience is important because it helps our soul in the process of progression?

Regarding those who believe that life's bad events are tests set up by God: They reason that if you fail the tests, you are refused entry into the Kingdom of Heaven. The problem with that concept is that we all do not have the same experiences and, therefore, the chance to make the same choices. Certainly, a soul that finds itself in the conditions of war is more likely to do evil things than one that experienced life as a nursery school teacher. So how can God judge one against another? One individual commits a terrible act in war, while the other individual was never given the opportunity to make the same mistake. Is one person given a free ticket to heaven while the other must jump many hurdles to gain entry?

Now consider an alternative view of the afterlife. What if the truly evil among us, upon death, move to a place reserved for soul repair? And what if the good among us progressed to the other side, find out that the other side is home, and discover that this life experience was a tutorial set up by the greatest teacher in the universe?

Perhaps we can change the paradigm that we use to view life. What if you couldn't lose the game of life? What if the events of life and this world were staged so that your soul could experience the event? What if you and God conducted your review on judgment day jointly after you pass over? What if God wanted you to do the life review knowing that you couldn't fool him anyway?

What if the people who do bad things were contributing to our soul achieving its mission here on Earth? The question is important enough to repeat: What if the people who did bad things actually served a function in God's plan? As others have stated it, interactions between human beings are never really between us and them; they are all between us and God. That is not to say that this world must have bad people, but when we no longer have bad people, our collective souls will have progressed past that experience.

It is important to remember that one could be told about pain and suffering, but until you experience pain and suffering you don't really understand it. One could be told about glory and fame, but you really don't understand it until you experience the adulation of others that accompany the experience along with the ancillary events that happen in those situations.

What if we chose the feelings that we wanted to experience in this life in a partnership with God prior to our arrival on the Earth? What if our true reality was not the Earth we are presently living in but the dimension we pass back to when we move on? And most importantly, what if we found that the bad times as well as the good times are the experiences that we actually sought when we came to Earth? Life is a full and complete experience. It is not enough to say that we are on this Earth to experience the good times; we are also on this Earth to experience the tough times.

Earth was created by the Lord to allow the soul to gain maturity through experience, and life exists for the soul to have experiences. Therefore, whatever happens during our lifetime has value because it provides the soul with the experiences it uses to learn and grow. A phrase that is popular today is quite appropriate for explaining the soul's learning: *It's all good.*

Secret:
The Soul Is Visible

The interesting thing is that we have accepted that the soul is invisible. The truth is that the soul is very visible. However in those who are drawn toward evil, the soul is difficult to see as it recedes into the body. The soul can be seen in the eyes of people. The soul's recession into the body can be seen as an absence in the eyes of those drawn to darkness.

There are people who have given up on truth and goodness and are living with a false set of values they have created. The values they have created always center on seeking power since they are lacking in personal power. Those individuals need to steal the soul energy of others because their soul has recessed, and as a result, produces less energy. Of course, one can't have a quality life without the soul being part of that life. Those individuals with soul regression will live a life permeated with pain. And when their souls pass on, they need to revisit the sickness in their soul and attempt to heal it before advancing in the plain of heaven.

Healthy souls need to either separate from these individuals or invest in them. Investing in sick souls means to reintroduce the light of goodness; but one must recognize the risk and the difficulty of the undertaking. Enough goodness over a long enough period of time has the ability to bring the soul back into the life of the individual. You'll know when that happens; you can see it in their eyes. But it is a long journey, albeit a noble one.

Edgar Cayce, as well as others, has talked about an aura of color that surrounds human beings. Although invisible to most of us, the aura is still there and is an indication of how the soul is feeling at any moment. It is important to remember that damaged individuals have had their soul recess into the body because of fear and misguided love. Their soul will not reemerge as a key component of life choices unless the fear can be quelled and the love can be reintroduced.

Secret:
Good Deeds Aren't about Getting Recognition, They're about Doing the Right Thing

Often people who do a good deed for someone expect a quid pro quo in the future—I did this for you, so you do something for me someday. If the person doesn't pay us back in some way, we are disappointed in them. In fact the chance to do a good deed is its own reward.

Think back on a time when you did a good deed. Most likely it made you feel better, and just as likely it probably was simply the right thing to do. When we are in a position to help someone, instead of expecting that person to repay *you,* you should ask him or her to repay the kindness to another person who needs a hand in the future. If you do that, not only will you have done something good but you may also be starting a cycle of goodness that propagates itself one good deed at a time. It's a mistake to think of a good deed as a favor that is owed a favor in return.

Parents frequently make this kind of mistake as their children grow into adulthood. One or both parents may believe that their kindness and self-sacrifice in raising their children earned them a reciprocal relationship when they grow older. However, it must be remembered parents make the sacrifices for the right reason, out of love for their children. They are not entitled to a payback when they get older as if the children owe a debt. Children do still need to take care of their parents in an appropriate way, not because they formally owe anything but because it is the right thing to do. Right thinking yields right action, and a righteous person is the result.

During my life as a school administrator I have been fortunate to be around some special people. It is my good fortune to work with Assistant Principal Bob Presland for many years. If you walked in on a conversation between Bob and a student in a disciplinary situation, he would invariably be saying, "You've got to do the right thing." It sounds simplistic, but it speaks volumes. We as human beings must put our objectives and philosophies in order, and then live by them. We all want others in the world to do the right thing, but we are less willing to set the example. Confucius said, "To put the world in order, we must first put the nation in order; to put the nation in order, we must first put the family in order; to put the family in order, we must first cultivate our personal life; we must first set our hearts right." As Bob would say, "We simply must do the right thing." The right thing is clear, and it doesn't need elaboration. It is simply the right thing.

Secret:
Our Soul Grows Through Service to Others

When our soul makes decisions, our life is wonderful. When our brain makes the decisions, it filters life through its experiences. Invariably, life decisions are based on cultural and social paradigms. When we make decisions separately from our soul, we are more likely to make decisions that hurt us and hurt others. This way of approaching life makes a more painful experience.

Dealing with life in a more meaningful and peaceful manner can be made a reality. It requires a trust in God, an understanding that human behavior is a result of conditions the soul lives in. Conditions refer to the context in which we make decisions. Conditions can be the type of home you were raised in, the kind of relationships you have had, the times in which you live, or the fatigue you may be feeling at the time a crucial decision has to be made. It is my hope that the secrets revealed in this book will offer a person the ability to make life decisions that are more meaningful and therefore will bring about a condition of joy.

We have been raised to believe that there is pure good and pure evil. Hence, it follows that evil is done by inherently evil souls and goodness is done by innately good souls. The problem with this idea is that it ignores the reality of life events. The many souls on Earth experience different life experiences, and each soul faces a different set of choices to make. It is easier for some souls to do good and others to do evil based on the conditions of the particular life. And yet it is inherent in all life experiences that making wise choices require forgiveness and understanding.

The most important secret to a more meaningful life is, "You have to like you." The best way to achieve liking our self is to do good for others. Remember, we always consider ourselves in terms of others. Think more of others, less of yourself, and begin enjoying a better life.

3. God and Man

Secret:
So, Tell Me about God...

The interesting thing about researching the feedback we have received from entities on the other side is the consistent difficulty in describing God. The common agreement that makes sense is that God is the creator of all things and has been best described as an entity of *pure love.*

The reality is that our mind's ability to understand is largely based on concepts and things that we have seen or experienced. Using our comparative experiences to understand all things, God is beyond our capacity to categorize and comprehend. There is simply nothing in our references to compare God to. As a result, we tend to create an image of a superman, someone sitting on a marble throne.

We tend to give the creator a face, a personality, and human characteristics. We think he is going to respond or act as the best of humankind would act. We are much more comfortable with God when we can assign him human characteristics to aid in our understanding.

The deal is that when we decide to come to Earth for a physical experience, we have agreed to forget much of what we knew on the other side or in our previous lives. This forgetfulness aids in our experiential learning during this lifetime. We have also forgotten what we knew about God and his existence on the highest level of heaven.

Regarding the unique importance of the physical universe, God has created multiple levels of entities, ranging from *spirit guides* to *angels,* to help us along in our learning experience. When we have interactions with the other side, it is likely God's agents who are helping, interacting, and guiding us, and not God directly. Even those who have died and returned to Earth after meeting "The Light" are unsure as to who "The Light" really was. In actuality, it appears "The Light" allows you to think he or she is whomever you would like to think he or she is.

We have a need to define God so that we can conceptualize the entity that is the creator. For all intents and purposes, think of God as the architect of all things. But just as an architect delegates tasks to builders, so does God. Not surprisingly, God does have a good number of excellent builders working for him.

Secret:
We Can Establish God's Relationship with Man

Simply stated we are connected to God at the Soul level. Therefore, all humanity is one at the soul level. God isn't testing us to see if we belong in the Kingdom of Heaven—he is letting us mature. Why he has chosen this path for maturing our soul, we can only ask—obviously at a later time. Perhaps as our soul progresses through heaven we won't have to ask, we will simply know. But God's relationship with man is all encompassing and if you ask if God is involved, the answer is always yes. If you ask why God would allow bad things to happen, the answer is that all things happen for a reason. If you want to know if God approves of something, look into your soul and you will get the answer. If the framework for the answer is love and forgiveness it has come from the soul. If the framework for the answer is not framed this way, it is coming from the strictly human experience, one that God intends us to learn from. The more we make decisions from the soul, the happier and more at peace we are.

It is also important to consider that we are of value to God as we live our experience. God has granted humankind free will as the strongest determiner of life's course. God certainly gets to live our experience with us and therefore is involved in billions of experiences every moment. It is also possible that at times, we human beings are putting on a good show.

God wants us to choose the right path and, as a loving creator, gives us the opportunity to learn from experience. But ultimately, what God wants us to learn is to love each other the way he loves us.

Secret:
Most of Us Question the Universe's Plan for Us At Times

We live our life experience with periods of pain, frustration, and discontent. It is reasonable to say that during these times we do not enjoy the lesson we are learning. Through the early part of my life, as with many people who have been pretty lucky, I believed that tragedy would always find another. I always believed that terrible things would never happen to me. I didn't really have a rational reason to believe I would always be so fortunate, but I still believed it. However, after being involved with tens of thousands of people as a teacher and a principal, I've learned that none of us go through life unscathed. Both as an educator dealing with people and in my own life, I've seen my fair share of suffering and loss. In my search to understand pain, fear, life and death, I have learned that we each have things to learn during our stay on Earth. I have come to understand that one of my jobs on this Earth as an educator and as an empathetic human being is to help others understand the pain of death and the confusion of life.

Life events need to be kept in their proper perspective, that is, the things that happen, have purpose. As we all know, at times we will not like what happens in our life, and at times, life can be very cruel. We live with this because we have no choice but to accept it as reality. During these times it is especially important to remember that there is a purpose to events happening that the Universe has intended. Perhaps, the bad times may be easier to accept if we keep things in perspective with this thought: If the Universe didn't find meaning in letting it happen, it wouldn't happen. We can continue to question the plan simply because we have trouble understanding that the events of our life are coordinating with a higher order. The higher order wants us to learn from experience, and therefore life comes with a full array of happenings, events, and moments.

Secret:
The Job Is Already Taken

Yes, your way is the right way to worship God as long as it doesn't hurt you or others. There was a point in the movie *"Oh, God!"* in which a puzzled character played by John Denver is trying to figure out why God picked him to be his messenger. Denver's character says to God, "I don't even belong to a church." God replies, "Neither do I."

Worship God in the way that warms your heart and allows you to accept the thoughts of others. Peace with God enables you to allow others to observe God in a different way, and this is a beautiful thing. Expecting people to worship God the way you see fit is not godly.

For those who kill in God's name, such as the fanatics who flew the planes that struck the Twin Towers, nothing is further from the soul than killing in God's name. If human beings want to do evil, they will do it. To do it in the name of God is the height of absurdity. And make no mistake about it; killing innocent civilians because of anger toward a government's policy is evil. God is incapable of evil and will never embrace such acts in his name.

As human beings, we have found it quite natural to stand in judgment of our fellow man. The problem is, the very act of standing in judgment of others is distancing one's soul from God. When we have condemned, has it really been in God's name or has it been a human action that is acting separately from the soul?

Let God do the judging. You do the living. If you want to play God, start by learning to forgive and love regardless of the circumstances. God does! And to all the fanatics across the country, and in the world, who are telling us to hate in his name: Stop playing God! The job is already taken.

Secret:
Humor Is One of God's Greatest Gifts

One of the best things to do in life is to find your sense of humor and learn to smile. As difficult as times may be, laughter helps. Woody Allen is one of those people who has a tendency to view the world in a cynical manner—funny but cynical. In his movie *Annie Hall* Alvy, the main character played by Allen himself, describes the world as consisting of people who are one of two types, either horrible or miserable. Those who are horrible are in wheelchairs, very sick, surrounded by death, and in similar situations. Allen described the rest as the miserable. In fact, Alvy states that we should be *thankful* if we are miserable! You *could* be horrible!

This philosophy came into play in my own life following the summer of 1992 when the school year came around. My colleagues at G.W. Hewlett High School had heard about our son's birth and the loss of our other son. Teachers returning to school looked at me as a person who had just lost one child and was either on the verge of losing another or, at the very least, facing the prospect of raising a severely handicapped child. On one occasion, I observed individuals at the end of the long main hallway of the school, and when they saw me they ran up a nearby staircase. It isn't that they were bad people, it's simply that they were people who couldn't deal with the tragedy surrounding me. They didn't know what to say around me, or how to say it. I called my wife and I told her about the incident in the context of the Woody Allen movie—we were no longer miserable, we had become horrible. And we laughed.

It is important to laugh and it is important not to hold others responsible for having trouble dealing with tragedy. Later on that first day of the school year, there was a knock on my door and both school psychologists came to see me. I laughed and said to them, "Now I *know* my life is crap; it takes two of you to come see me."

I don't know how Woody Allen would describe the next phase because it turned out quite differently than people expected. In a period of months we went from being among "the horrible" to being the recipients of a miracle when David came home healthy and well. My wife and I were no longer "the horrible," but we couldn't imagine seeing ourselves as "the miserable" in any way. So I guess we have to be careful regarding the philosophies of others. Woody Allen can be quite observant of human behavior, but there is a balance in life that we also need to recognize. It isn't all horrible and miserable, sometimes it is wonderful, and when you can laugh through the tough times, that makes it all a little better.

4. Learning the Major Lessons of Life: Love, Fear, Evil, and Forgiveness

Secret:
Fear Is the Opposite of Love

Neale Donald Walsch in the book *Conversations with God* states that God believes we either come from a place of love or a place of fear. Whenever we make decisions based on fear, whenever we speak based on fear, whenever we act based on fear, we are moving away from the soul progression we have come to Earth to master. Government, schools, and bureaucracies in general come from a place of fear. They make rules to control people based on neurotic responses to past events. For example, schools have created comprehensive systems of discipline to control children. These systems fail in every school in which love is not present. Perhaps, if they spent more time making a user friendly environment that children loved being in, they wouldn't have to worry so much about discipline. Healthy companies, healthy institutions, healthy organizations have been able to overcome fear and come from a place of love.

An inability to deal with fear can rob a person of his life. Not being able to deal with fears isn't thought of as a major disability, but it should be. People have an enormously difficult time overcoming fear. We are all afraid of some things, and more likely, many things. The hardest thing for us to do is to face our fears head on. Most of us try to avoid dealing with the fear or situations in which the fear will arise.

We often avoid taking action because of our fears. We, of course want absolute assurance that our future is secure. But imagine that each step you took in the world was fraught with danger because you could neither see nor hear. Would you be afraid to walk and move forward? Helen Keller said the following about security, "It does not exist in nature, nor do the children of men as a whole experience it. Avoiding danger is no safer in the long run than outright exposure. Life is either a daring adventure or nothing." I would add that you should not take risks foolishly, but don't be afraid to take risks for your dreams. If you trust your inner voice, you will be able to differentiate between foolishness and risks worth taking.

It is important to consider the true risk in actions to be taken. Based on a true assessment of realities, decide not to be be foolish, but don't let fear unfairly compromise your experience on this Earth. Again, as with all life experience, deal with action in balance. Too much or too little is not the way to go.

It is important to remember that with enough energy and courage, we can accomplish great things. Since we ultimately can't avoid fear, run away from it, or outthink it, our best strategy is confronting fear and defeating it to the best of our ability. The antidote to fear is love. So, as with all things, we must be compassionate to ourselves. Fears are often deeply rooted and chronic. Attempt to work past them, but be kind to yourself during your journey. Fear is a very tough opponent, and it is important to remember that courage is going forward in spite of our fears. Do your best, but do not be discouraged if you do not succeed at first.

The secret is to decide which fears are robbing you of the life experiences you desire. Once these fears are recognized, a plan should be formulated to help deal with the problem. It may include therapy, self-help books, or strength borrowed from a friend or loved one. The more that love is part of the solution, the quicker that fear can be defeated.

We don't know when life will go our way, and we don't know when life will not. But we are fully capable of stealing our own lives by worrying about it. Stop worrying and get on with the business of living. One thing is for sure, worry and fear never made anything better. Love and optimism make everything better!

Secret:
Courage Is Going Forward Despite Being Afraid

Quite simply, we all admire, want, and desire courage. I love the quote from Ambrose Redmoon on courage that says, "Courage is not the absence of fear, but rather the judgment that something else is more important than fear." We are all afraid of things, but it is crucial that we recognize that we are not alone. Fear is a common element that all people must deal with.

Ralph Waldo Emerson said, "Whatever you do, you need courage. Whatever course you decide upon, there is always someone to tell you that you are wrong. There are always difficulties arising that tempt you to believe your critics are right." I believe that we need to have the courage to risk making mistakes. Somewhere in our upbringing, the concept that we will make many mistakes and have failures was left out. But we need to remember that if we let failure stop us, none of us would have learned to walk. Walking like many things we do in our life begins with falling on our face: frequently.

Again, fear is the opposite of love. Human beings often do bad things when we are afraid and we do worse things when an entire community, society or country is afraid. As a result of our collective failure to deal with fear, we live in a very fragile world that is threatened by a catastrophe that will be of our own making, one resulting from a simple misunderstanding among nations. World War I broke out when the Czar of Russia and his cousin, the Kaiser of Germany were scared of the next action of the other. The Czar started moving his troops to the German border because he feared his cousin would attack. The Kaiser attacked because his cousin was moving troops to the border.

I believe it is important to go through life with the thought quoted from Ambrose Redmoon present in our mind: "Courage is not the absence of fear, it is doing what you have to do in spite of your fear." It is equally important to remember that the antidote to fear is love and understanding. And in love we are all connected at the soul level.

It is crucial that we recognize our world is a result of our collective consciousness. The reason we have a world with so much scarcity, war, separateness, disasters and natural disasters is a result of a world dominated by fear. Lack results in conflict and problems among humankind. What we worry about, we tend to draw into our world. When we approach the world in a loving way, we work together to solve the problems of our planet and manifest good things into our world.

When the collective consciousness of humankind centers on love, the Earth can be a Garden of Eden. But it will take a human race that trusts love and recognizes hate and fear as enemies of humankind.

Secret:
Accept Criticism When it Comes From a Loving Place

Like most people, I don't like to be criticized. In fact, like some, I have been known to loudly argue my case. However, I endorse the principles that Richard Carlson laid out in his advice book for men. Sometimes you just need to stop talking, stop defending yourself and listen. There will be plenty of time to refute matters that you disagree with or to correct false statements. Additionally, not every comment is worthy of a response. Sometimes the loudest way to voice disagreement is with a stern look and stark silence. When you find yourself in an argument with friends and loved ones, just stop arguing and practice listening. Most likely, the verbal defense you offer is natural and does not need any practice. The art of listening may allow you to self-correct; at the very least it will give you time to organize your thoughts. Sometimes you just need to shut up. If the critic is right, you will have just learned something; if the critic is wrong there is plenty of time and numerous ways to refute the comment. Just remember some critics can't be corrected, and at least their opinion is free, which makes it worth the cost.

Futurist Joel Barker, illustrates a pitfall of being too quick to defend oneself against a perceived insult. In the story a man is out for a drive on a beautiful day on a winding road. Then from around a curve, a woman comes driving straight at him and at the last minute, curves back into her own lane. As she passes the man, she leans out of the car and yells, "Pig!" The man is incredulous that this woman who almost killed him dare yell an insult at him. He leans out his window and yells back, "Hog!" and proceeds down the road satisfied that he got the last word on this rude woman. He then drives around the curve and hits a group of pigs that were in the road. He heard an insult when he should have listened to a warning.

The man in this story was afraid that someone would get the better of him. His rush to judgment blinded him to a message of love. The other motorist was afraid he would get hurt. We can always think more clearly when we come from a place of love and we leave our defensive nature in the past. Sometimes criticism is designed to realign our soul with its purpose.

Ultimately, people who do not allow criticism to be given from people, do not get the opportunity to recorrect mistakes before they are made. The real question about criticism is whether or not it is coming from a loving place. If it is, accept it with open arms.

Secret:
God Doesn't Allow Evil to Exist, Man Does

As I mentioned previously, as a young child I was intellectually able to comprehend the acts of Hitler and Nazi Germany. But emotionally, I was at a loss to understand why people would kill innocents, especially children. I wondered, in my naïve childhood mind, what could have gone so wrong to turn citizens of a highly civilized country into evil monsters? For many years as an adult, I wondered the same thing.

As I went on my search about the secrets of life and death, I can now offer some insights into why God allows evil to exist on the Earth. First of all, it is not God who allows evil to exist, it is man. God allows man to shape the Earth and its experience. It is hard to imagine that there is a real function for an Adolf Hitler or a Sadaam Hussein or the other characters that have hurt so many people. But as we unfold the secrets of life and the reasons we are on Earth, it is understandable why these monsters exist. They serve as a force to help us understand good by contrasting it with evil. They create an experience for the soul as it triumphs over wrong. In short, their evil gives the world contrast and allows our soul to learn through experience.

Again, God does not bring evil onto the Earth, man does. Why do some people create evil, embrace evil, and become evil? Simply put, evil is separation from the creator—the further the soul journeys away from the creator the more evil it becomes. Souls separate from the creator through the succumbing to fear. Evil comes about from fear, the direct opposite of love—and love is the creator. The greater the degree of fear the soul experiences the more it needs to stop the fear. The problem is that without appropriate guidance, souls in fear get lost and journey down the wrong road. The right road is to return back to love and to the creator. However, souls in pain are drawn to the immediate need to control. The human brain tells the soul that control of the situation is the way to alleviate pain, and to get control it needs power over other people. Since the soul is in so much pain and the most immediate need is to end the pain, the soul will do anything to gain power and thereby control its environment.

Lost souls are sure that the journey down the road to power in search of the land of control is the way to achieve peace, meaning, and joy. On this road, the soul gets momentary illusions of control. It feels that it has ultimate power when it commits evil acts because the soul has created an environment in which it pretends that it is the creator. This momentary pleasure is sufficient to gratify the soul so the soul continues to seek other moments like it. As time goes on the soul realizes it has gone down the wrong road and has embarked on a lifetime of evil. However, by then the soul is so far down the road, it cannot find the way back. It is also a soul in a terrible state of fear. It is terrified of venturing back to the creator and facing a life review based on evil.

The soul in fear needs power to gain control over others. Therefore, we find many of these souls in leadership positions in education, business, and politics. Souls in fear will pay an incredibly high price to gain power because they see it as a way to relieve their fear through control. These souls are making the world a more difficult place for healthy souls. However, they also create a great test for those with healthy souls to exercise love and forgiveness. It is a test because to seek payback from a soul that hurt us or a loved one is one of the most seductive forces on Earth. The more evolved soul learns to let it go.

However, we need to recognize the root of evil lies with the free will of damaged souls. When we learn to treat each other with love, we will starve the fire that is needed to create evil. Edgar Cayce stated that everyone has the capacity to be good, evil is never a given.

Secret:
There Is a Method for Defeating Evil on this Earth

The tough thing about defeating evil is recognizing its weakness. Evil disguises where it has weakness and is good at getting others to emulate its behavior. When good people employ evil behaviors to defeat evil people, evil wins. Evil is separation from God. When we separate from God to defeat those who have already separated from God, we have lost our way.

What we must recognize is that evil can't stand the light of day. The light of day is exposure. Evil wants to operate in the shadows of fear. Evil is like a vampire that can't tolerate the glare of sunlight exposing its lack of soul. We do not defeat evil by bringing in darkness; we defeat evil by bringing in the light. It is important to clarify an evil soul from a soul doing bad things. An evil soul is so lost it cannot find its way back to God. A soul doing bad things is confused and can be recorrected through understanding. Abraham Lincoln said, "If I turn my enemy into my friend, have I not won?" It is important to know if you are working with a life force that can be reached (most can) or a life force that is on Earth to bring in evil (which is rare, but real). In either case, fight through love; do not become evil in your pursuit to destroy evil. That doesn't mean that we have to be pacifist, it means that as we fight we must keep our moral center. We must remember that evil as a force conquers through the act of recruitment. Again, when we become evil to defeat evil, evil wins.

Since evil exists on Earth as a contrast with good, we need to understand evil and we need to understand good. Understanding evil helps complete the maturation of our soul. Without evil, what would good reject? However, evil can be eradicated from Earth. It will happen when the collective soul has matured and mastered its lessons. In other words, humanity understands that we are all in this together. This will be when humanity recognizes the greater good is not about self-interest it is about helping all souls' have a better life. That day could be today if we choose it to be!

Secret:
Forgiveness Is Healthy

Probably the most difficult philosophy of life to live by is to forgive those who attack us or try to hurt us. I came across an article by Thich Nhat Hanh entitled "Arrows into Flowers." The title deserves attention. The article is an excerpt from his book *Creating True Peace* and begins with the story of Buddha the night before his enlightenment. Mara, the Evil One, attacks him with thousands of arrows from his army. As the arrows fly closer to him, they turn into flowers and fall harmlessly at his feet. Hanh stresses with this parable that it is possible to water the seed of compassion even in a situation of adversity. He suggests that we can render the arrows aimed at us useless through compassion for our attackers. He states that our attackers fire arrows that come from their pain. Certainly, this is a life lesson that needs much effort to embrace, but it can't hurt to start small and grow it over time.

Research into health continually reveals the importance of practicing the art of forgiveness. Those who forgive tend to live longer and healthier lives. Imagine that doing the right thing not only helps you be happier and healthier but also helps you live longer.

The Dalai Lama tells the story of a monk who was imprisoned by the Chinese for over twenty years. When the Dalai Lama asked him if he was ever afraid, the monk responded, "Yes, twice." The Dalai Lama then asked what he was afraid of, and the monk responded that on two occasions he almost lost his compassion for his captors.

Forgiveness stands in opposition to some of our cultural practices. But it does stand in alignment with our religious training. An eye for an eye, the original Hebrew justice system was actually meant to be kind. It meant that a man should not have his arm cut off for stealing a loaf of bread. The punishment should be commensurate with the act. Christ said that we should turn the other cheek. In other words a man, who steals a loaf of bread, may in fact be doing it because his family is starving. Work on forgiving others, and you and the world will be better off for it. It is hard at first, but like many things, it gets easier in time.

Secret:
Love Is the Greatest Force in the Universe

We all want to live our lives with more love, peace, and meaningfulness. The root of all that is good can be found in love. The soul emanates love, we are most connected with God when we love, we live in a state of peace when we love, and we find the road to meaningfulness through love.

In our society we have limited the use of the word *love.* We have dozens of variations of bad phrases to spread hurt and discouragement. But we are still reliant on one word of total appreciation, one word that embodies the life spirit given from God, one word: *love.*

This is life's special secret: Live in a state of love with the human race, the Earth, and all living creatures. The reward is a life of splendid magnificence.

As a high school principal I was able to have calm buildings that were disciplined and free of violence. I believe it was an outgrowth of the fact that the students knew that their principal loved them and wanted their life to be the best it could be. My administrative staff had to love kids or they wouldn't be happy in my system. You can't bluff kids for long. If you tell young people that something is being done in their best interest and it is really not, they will see through the hypocrisy. Love had to be more than a word; love had to be a feeling that ran through their world. As each school year began, I met with the students in assemblies for each grade level. I told them that I loved them, and they were going to be treated as if they were my own sons and daughters. I suggest that principals around the country say it, walk it, and live it. Furthermore, we got the best results because the discipline came from a loving place. When students did the wrong thing and faced punishment, they knew that the disciplinary measures were set by an administration that loved them and didn't want to hurt them. An administration that enjoys punishing children or feels they deserve to be hurt will be exposed in time.

If you are looking for a magic cure for all that ails you, all that is wrong with society, and all that is wrong with the world, all you have to do is learn to truly love others.

In Summary

The Secret of Why We Are on Earth and What God Wants of Us

We are on Earth to learn lessons that are difficult to master on the other side. Our soul knows all there is to know, but it cannot fully make sense of that knowledge because it lacks experience. All in all, our soul is concerned with experiential growth and that is why we are here on Earth. Our soul can and does grow in heaven, but it can grow much faster with the earthly experience. We are here for the purpose of our soul's growth.

Our stay on Earth is very much like a student leaving home to go study at a university. Our time on Earth is real, but it is not our true home. We are temporarily relocated here to learn. We are not meant to stay at the university once our studies are completed, and the same is true for our stay on Earth. Once our soul has gained the experiences it came to gain, it is released and returns to heaven.

Each soul has different experiences during its visit to Earth. Some souls are learning more advanced lessons based on their past development. Given that we are here for the soul to gain experience, we can begin to understand why there is good and evil in the world. With both, the soul gets experience and that is what God intended as Earth is dominated by immature souls. In fact, if you think of the time spent on Earth as very brief in the context of heaven, our time on Earth is much more of a quick study than we might have otherwise thought.

God created the Earth so our soul can learn from its experience here. The soul is of God and it is He in us. Individuals who have gone through incredibly painful experiences and live in pain are not very likely to accept such a simple explanation. They will certainly reject that they could or would have any part in planning a life that would have such awful experiences.

But consider: To know intuitively and to experience are far different things. The soul already knows about pain and joy, love and heartbreak; however, it does not fully grasp the context until it has been given the chance to live through a variety of events. Life experiences of all kinds are what the soul needs—good, bad, and horrible. And that is why we spend this time on Earth.

God would like our life experience to evolve to kindness, forgiveness, and selflessness—and result in the soul's growth. God wants us to experience, grow, and learn. God wants us to know the meaning of things on the experiential level. God wants us to return to heaven with a more mature soul, one that has grown through its time on Earth.

God wants our soul to adopt more godlike qualities of forgiveness, unconditional love for others, and oneness with each other and the Universe. Each lifetime on Earth that brings us closer to those ideals is a successful one. However, we always need to remember that even a life of mistakes helps our soul to grow. God won't let this lifetime be a failure for any of us. Each stay on Earth allows our soul to learn, even if the experiences are different than the lessons we had desired to learn. However, through many lives the soul learns a multitude of lessons and progresses.

The truth is that during our time on Earth, we want more from God than he requires of us. His desire for us is simple and elegant. He wants our soul to grow through experience and move toward the values that are inherent in our soul. The pace by which our soul grows varies. But God puts no pacing clock on us; the degree our soul grows with each stay on Earth is fine with God. All things have been created for the soul to learn—at its own pace.

Secrets of Life

Part III

Creating a Better Life:
How to Live Your Life with More
Joy, Meaningfulness and Peace

1. Choices and Approaches to Life

Secret:
All Our Decisions Are Based on Our Foundation Values

One of the biggest mistakes we make as we proceed down the road of life is that we rarely revisit the intellectual foundations we base our life on, our values. If you think about it, virtually every choice we make is based on a value-driven thought derived from a firm belief we have about the world. All the roles we choose to play are based on our value structure, and they are all based on our belief system of what is right and wrong.

As we are growing up, we acquire beliefs that become the core foundation for the choices we make and the actions we take. Our beliefs guide the choices we make and as a result create our life experience. We acquire these core beliefs in a variety of ways. Our parents teach us some of the values we take through life. Other values we acquire from society. We learn about the world through movies, television, books, music, relationships, the random and not so random observations we make, the lessons we learn in school, from religious institutions, the media, and more. Multiple sources contribute to the foundation we rely on to make our decisions throughout life. The foundation blocks (our values and beliefs) become the defining instrument of our life and determine what type of people we become. The more sources that validate the belief, the stronger the value becomes in our approach to the world.

The things we have come to believe as core values are deeply ingrained in our behavior and will remain so unless a strong outside force or life circumstance causes us to reconsider our approach to the world. Absent a major event in life, foundation beliefs remain fairly consistent throughout a lifetime. When the foundation blocks are morally and ethically solid and inherently positive and aligned with a core spiritual belief, the individual has the right ingredients for a positive life. These individuals have a greater tendency to be happy and contribute to the community of humankind. These individuals will have a better chance of standing strongly through the storms of life that all human beings encounter. On the other hand, when the foundation blocks have cracks in wisdom, are morally or ethically lacking, devoid of an appropriate barometer regarding where the individual's life fits in with others and the universe, or is inherently negative, the soul is in for a rough life. And for that matter, everyone who encounters that soul is in for a very negative experience. The more misdirected the core beliefs, the more a life will be misaligned and the greater the chance for a painful experience on Earth.

From time to time in our lives, it is beneficial to revisit the core values utilized in making life choices. Start by making a list of the things that are most important to you and attempt to trace where the value came from. Be sure to visit your parents' core values. Whether we like it or not, our beliefs are frequently based on an acceptance or rejection of what our parents exposed us to. Common sense can often mislead us in determining what we will reject from our childhood experience. For example, a child who witnessed great violence in the home would be thought to reject that type of situation in the future. But research indicates that a person who has witnessed outrageous behavior in the home frequently mimics that behavior as an adult.

Before you consider reviewing your values and beliefs, you may want to ask yourself a few pointed questions: What in your life makes you happy and what makes you unhappy? What are (or were) your parents' core values and what is their relationship to your values? Are your core values centered on the approval of others or doing what your soul knows to be the right thing? Have your core values given you the life that you want? In general, are you happy or unhappy with your everyday life? Are you excited about the future? Would you want your child to live life with the same degree of happiness you experience? If you don't like the answers, you can look to build a new foundation. Start by understanding the most important rule of happiness: We must like ourselves to be happy—and we like ourselves most when we help others.

When you buy a house, there is a reason why an engineer would have you shy away from one with a cracked foundation. Fixing a damaged foundation is difficult and usually time consuming. This is true whether we are talking about a house or a life. For human beings, the process of change is difficult, it requires much effort and, most importantly, time and patience. You must remember that over the course of a lifetime, your values and beliefs have become who you are. Changing your values and beliefs is changing you as a person. However, few things you undertake in life can change the course you are on with more beneficial results.

Secret:
Set Up the Game of Life So That You Win

So many people set up their life as a game they can never win. Subconsciously and culturally we are stacking the cards against our own happiness. No money is enough, no promotion is good enough, no accomplishment is meaningful enough because of the way we approach our life. If we objectively consider the rules of our game, we would realize that no matter how many runs we score, we will always fall short.

The Dalai Lama talks of the unhappiness of many people because they are always living in desire for the next thing. They are permanently in a state of "lack". Culturally, this has become the dominant trend in many modern societies. Whatever we have, we want more, we need more and the joy we receive from accomplishments and possessions are short lived.

If we have a home and a car we want more money in the bank. If we have more money in the bank we want a stock portfolio. If we have a large stock portfolio, we are envious of the next guy who has a bigger portfolio... and so it goes. Whatever we have, we set up the game of life to be a losing hand.

We have forgotten that life is about being happy. We have somehow constituted our value structure to subjugate happiness to virtually everything else. In this broken value structure, what you have has become more important than who you are and how you behave in the world community.

We each need to set up our personal game of life so that we win. We win when we treat others well and like ourselves. We win when we laugh and enjoy life. We win when we set up the rules of our game of life based on happiness.

When it comes to life, if we expect too much of ourselves, we are chasing a finish line that is constantly moving away from us and can never be reached. On the other hand, if we ask too little of ourselves, we will fail to accomplish what we are capable of achieving. Our expectations of ourselves directly affect the life we live. Given the choice of life expectations, I frequently think of the saying, "A ship is safest in the harbor." But ships were not built to stay in the harbor. The same is true for life. Life is an adventure and we should seek much from ourselves. The trick is to have appropriate values as to what true accomplishment is and to go about life in good spirit.

Most of us are comfortable turning life into a game that we think can be won or lost. Life is an adventure and whatever your soul receives in this lifetime is a success. Try to make the world a better place and accomplish many things. But there is no profit in beating yourself up over not reaching a goal that was arbitrary in the first place.

The people who take the position that life is a game to be won are playing a game they can, ironically, never win. These folks keep moving the bar up no matter what they achieve. They are perpetually unhappy because they have created a game that they can't win. Amazing isn't it? We are capable of creating a game in which we are the only player, and we still can't win. These individuals fear contentment as something that will steal their fire and prevent them from accomplishing the next great feat.

It is perfectly acceptable to set the bar to drive yourself to great heights, but don't move the bar to the point in which you are never happy. Since you are creating the rules of the game, let yourself win once in a while.

Secret:
Make a Life Plan That Includes Joy

John Lennon's song "Beautiful Boy (Darling Boy)" has a famous and often quoted line "Life is what happens to you while you're busy making other plans." It expresses what happens so often to so many. Regardless of the good and bad breaks we get in life, most people really haven't considered how they want to approach their life. One important thing people can do to improve their lives is to decide on a *philosophy of living.*

Generally, people do not have a game plan, they do not think about life as a gift or as a great adventure. For a moment, think of life as sort of a gigantic amusement park that you are visiting for about eighty years. However, there are a thousand years worth of rides and attractions, and rather than taking a little time to look at a map and planning your visit based on your philosophical outlook, on what you enjoy and what you want to learn, you simply get on whatever ride is next. You will have "an experience," and it may actually turn out to be a good one, but you have better odds of enjoying and learning from your experience if you design it based on your philosophy of living.

People tend to live their life, expecting to reflect on that life at the end of it, at a point in which we can change nothing about the choices we've made. This is life happening to us, rather than us shaping a life for ourselves. Having a philosophy in mind to help guide us through our life makes it more likely that our time on Earth will be meaningful. We are all passing through this world and we are here for a limited time. It is important to decide what we want to learn, contribute, and experience during our stay.

The philosophy that I have chosen for my life is to learn as much as possible and to try and leave every place I go a little better than I found it. I suggest the same philosophy to others. Can you imagine how wonderful this world would be if hundreds of millions of people left the world a little better than they found it?

Wouldn't it be incredible if this were the universal way of living? Many of us talk a good game about improving the world, but on the whole, we just don't do a very good job of following up.

We do take the good and bad karma we have earned during our stay on Earth back to the other side. Our philosophy of living should be based on the concept of making numerous contributions to others and to the world at large. After all, everything we do is really between God and us, and we do take what the soul learns and all its growth with us. Remember, don't do the right thing for a reward in the afterlife, do it because it is the right thing to do. Come up with a philosophy of living based on what you want to get out of life, and then *give to life*.

The choice is ours, we are going down the road one way or another: Do you want to design your trip or let the trip take you? It is actually easier for people who are unhappy to change because their need for a different life is more apparent. However, everyone would benefit from some redesign of our life plan based on adopting a philosophy of living that takes into account what we want to get and give in this lifetime.

Secret:
The Universe's Design for the Stages of Life

Actually, aging is a pretty cool idea. As human beings we accept the realities of life without questioning it a great deal. For example, we age and move through different life cycles during a lifetime. We don't think about why it is so because it is natural and it is a reality for all of us. The fantasy of the novel *The Picture of Dorian Gray* plays with the idea of what would happen if we do not age, but even that story ultimately ends in disaster.

When life was created on Earth, all creatures were given a cycle of aging—the fruit fly, the tree, and the human being all age. Most of us never think about why the Creator designed life this way, so perhaps we should take a moment and reflect. Why did he design a life cycle with an expiration date?

Let's consider the good thing about aging. We get to experience many phases of life from different vantage points. Those of us who live to old age get to be babies and teenagers; we get to be young and vital and twenty; we experience the changes of middle age and the time for reflection that is afforded the elderly. If the idea of life is to gain experience so the soul can mature, aging by its very design is a pretty interesting concept.

The adult stages of life, when we have the greatest freedom to choose our own path to gaining experience, break down into three periods. Our twenties and thirties is the time we have to build a life. A good description of this time of life is that we have so far to go and we are rarely satisfied with the progress we have made. In contrast, middle age is a time when we can reflect and look forward, all at the same time. We can stop to consider if we like our past life choices, and if we don't, there is still time to do something about it. Finally, our senior years are a time when we can use the wisdom gained throughout our earlier periods in life. Of course, if we choose to be negative, we can dwell on growing old as a time in which our body is becoming less reliable and our mind more forgetful. But using wisdom born of our earlier life experience, old age can be a blessing—if we choose to make it so. Like everything else, it is very much about what we want to do with the choices we have at every stage of life.

In our twenties and thirties we can get obsessive about our own success. We can spend a good deal of time measuring our success in comparison with that of others during these years. This kind of comparison is not a good barometer of our own experience, but it is the one we almost always use. Additionally, this is the time in which we must adjust to changes: living on our own, marrying and living with another, having children and coping with the demands on our time that come with becoming a parent and staking out a career.

Given our hopes for success, frequently the career we choose doesn't proceed exactly as planned and we end up investing an enormous amount of energy and emotion in dealing with an obsession on our career and desire for success. It is good to remember that what is considered important is frequently culturally biased. Our culture tends to measure success in terms of wealth. As a result, in our society we value making a lot of money regardless of how you do it. The social worker, teacher, or nurse is frequently viewed as not quite fully successful in life solely because of their less than maximal income potential. That is not only an example of cultural bias, it is an example of the worst kind of value that has been transferred to us during the socializing process of youth.

Many people during their twenties and thirties see themselves, falsely, as being less than they truly are. The secret to breaking out of it is to stop, take a breath, and reprogram your brain. You have a great deal of life to live, so start by identifying your values and determine whether you are living according to values that are truly important to you. This time of life is a wonderful time to create a life plan: Make a plan and follow it.

In middle age, when we get to reflect on the choices we have made, we can see if life has gone as planned or we have somehow strayed. Problems appear in middle age when you don't like what you see upon reflection and feel that your future is limited. It is important to remember that many people have done their finest work after their middle years. Try to think of middle age as one more step in a great adventure rather than a time for regrets. In life all choices lead to an experience, and our soul learns from experience. Try and consider that if in middle age you reflect on experiences that haven't been pleasant—your soul has nevertheless gained a great deal of insight through the experience. No experience is really a waste of time, nor is any experience wasted on our soul. As you should do in all stages of life, decide what you want to do from this point on.

In our senior years the soul continues to gain from experience, but life also becomes about the experience for others who are witnessing this time in a person's life. The elderly have much to contribute and much to enjoy. As a senior citizen we may have more flextime than we had in our younger years, and it is crucial to identify meaningful activities to pursue. My mother and father were great examples of experiencing life fully as seniors. In his eighties, my father continued to fight for medical benefits for returning war veterans. My mother also worked on a variety of charitable efforts, as she had all her life. It is great to get up each morning and contribute to the world around us.

Remember, the Universe designed life to include aging as a way for the soul to gain experience. In the early time of life when we are making a life plan, it is good to keep in mind that life is not about arriving, it is about the journey, and at this age the journey is pretty special. And it is also good to remember that all journeys eventually come to an end, and the key question you will ask after the journey is over will be; did you make a difference along the way? Be sure to include that thought in your life plan.

When we reflect back on life in our middle age years, there are often things we regret. That is fine: Few lives turn out the way people think they were going to turn out. Just remember that tomorrow is there for the taking, and it begins with your choices today.

Go get it, and if your journey takes you somewhere other than you thought you were going, that is the human experience. Welcome to it and enjoy the ride.

In the senior years the best experience is one in which important endeavors are identified and pursued. Like in other stages of life, one must seize the moment and decide the best thing to do each day. Senior citizens should do what's important—read to children, plant flowers, start important projects, write memoirs, enjoy the sunsets to come.

The contributions we make and the love we experience throughout our life is based on the choices we make. If we live with good humor, grace and concern for others, life can be wonderful in every stage.

Secret:
Real Change Is Possible

We all know that for the human race and for individuals, certain problems never seem to go away. Solutions are hard to come by for two reasons. The first is that we want the issues we face to be fixed right now, and we are generally too impatient to do the long-term work that true solutions require. The second reason is that problem solving often requires us to do something differently. In most cases, we don't want to change; we want someone else to change. Unfortunately, if we don't do anything differently, we are going to get pretty much the same results we are getting now.

If the problem you face involves creating a different behavior in someone else, the question to ask is, do they want to change? It is very much like the story of why adults and children go to a psychologist. An adult goes to a psychologist because the adult wants help; a child goes because the adult wants help. Obviously the better results are likely to be gained by the party who admits there is a problem. If you want another person to change their behavior, you can forget about it until he or she acknowledges it and owns the problem. You can make things better in your life by approaching what you can do differently, then doing it.

If life is filled with problems and regret, declare your life a do-over. You can't change the portions of your life that you have already lived, but you can start all over from today. Look at your problems as an opportunity to have a new and exciting start.

In the movie *City Slickers*, one of the main characters has made a mess of his life. Even though he is an adult, he and his two friends decide that his life is a do-over. The same decision can be made by anyone, if you life isn't working for you, declare a do-over. But in this do-over, *decide that you are going to be happy*. Do the things that make you feel good and will make you become a better person. The better you are as a person, the more you will like yourself. The more you like yourself, the more successful the do-over.

Secret:
Wisdom Is the Guiding Light to All Things

When speaking to the average American, we find many people are disappointed with the choices we have in our leadership regardless of their political affiliation. Our governmental leaders are constantly making poor decisions because they have been educated in a society in which perspective and honor have been relegated to the bottom tier of priorities. Western society has confused intelligence with wisdom. When it comes to decision making, wisdom is the most important quality a human being can have. Wisdom is the kind of understanding that is gained through experience that has been combined with intelligence, instinct, and spiritual connection. When wisdom is applied to decision making, good decisions ensue, which are accompanied by positive outcomes. Wisdom is the crucial ingredient for success whether it is in leadership or life. Wisdom is what we seek in others when we have to make a crucial choice regarding which road in life we should pursue.

Unfortunately, to some degree, wisdom has become a casualty of our modern culture. Rarely do we tell the young to seek answers from those who have lived long and learned well. We know that wisdom is not assured by age, position, or professional success. The older we are, the more experiences we have for reference, the greater the chance that a person may be wise. But there is no guarantee that the lessons of life have been learned and that neurotic fears have not taken hold.

If we are to teach the young to become wise, it begins with observation, questioning and reading. We do not have to accept the views of others in our research, but we do have to consider them. The young are given the gift of youth, a quick mind, and a strong body. The older we get, the less our body responds to our commands, and the slower our mind reacts to tasks. However, aging does bring the experience that is helpful in creating reflective wisdom.

Acquiring wisdom, like all things that are worth something, takes a combination of God's natural gifts and recognition that it is a valuable commodity to be sought and valued. We have the intelligence to process what is learned and the curiosity and desire to study life and its inner meanings. These actions are positive steps in recognizing the value of wisdom.

We often wish that our children were smarter and that they would make better decisions. However, good choices are a result of wisdom. The same is true for us; I would wish upon you the gift of wisdom as you age. It will help you age gracefully and allow you to contribute fully to the world around you. But wisdom demands we reflect on our life choices. Wisdom makes us question the conventional and examine the unpopular. If allowed, wisdom can help a lost world find its way back to a path it was meant to take. In a world dominated by wisdom, we all understand that we are connected at the soul level.

Secret:
Overwhelmed? Make a List and Learn to Let Go

We commonly consider the negative happenings of our life as fate or as a punishment for wrongdoings from this or another life. Many people are hard on themselves for mistakes they make. If we lose money on an investment, we feel that we should have known better. If we screw up a relationship, we question what is wrong with us. For many, accepting our human failings is very difficult.

Deep down inside we are all really little boys and girls who are trying to make it through in this world. We can act mature and we often are, but we still have the core fears that we had when we were young. We feel we are in over our heads whenever we finally recognize that we are vulnerable—something that children recognize immediately but adults try to suppress. The secret to attaining the optimum enjoyment of the time we spend on Earth—even those times when it seems we are fighting for survival—is to recognize that our life is all part of a bigger plan. When we are most down on ourselves remember that human failings come as part of the package in gaining life experience. We all feel overwhelmed at times; some just handle it better than others. The soul learns from the negative and the positive, indeed from all experiences.

It may help to acknowledge that life places great pressures on us. Everybody feels pressure, and everybody has trying experiences and difficult choices to make. If one believes that life is happenstance and there is no reason for all the bad things, life can be a very hard pill to swallow. Individuals who have a faith in a spiritual presence and believe things are happening for a reason have a much easier time in dealing with the ups and downs of life.

One suggestion on handling pressure is when you are feeling overwhelmed, sit down and make a list of the things that are concerning you. Next to each of your concerns, write down your options. This very act will help to remove pressure. It is funny, but for some reason our brain seems to think if we do not express our preoccupation with problems, somehow we will forget it. We should be so lucky. Problems that aren't discussed stay on our mind and wear us down. Write them down, synthesize solutions or actions to take, and then let them go. If the answer to a problem is not apparent, leave it to the subconscious to work on it as you go about your life.

You will also feel less overwhelmed when you consider that one day after we have learned the lessons that we were supposed to learn, we will go home to the other side where no one is over-whelmed. On this side, from time to time, being overwhelmed is just part of the deal. Make a list and leave it to your subconscious to work on it. You will feel better.

And if anything on the list is just an obsession about past events that can't be changed, consider that what has happened in life was supposed to happen so the soul could learn and experience. We are so sure that this mess on Earth is reflective of a universe out of control, but what if the universe makes perfect sense? What if God made life on Earth a certain way but gave us the ability to alter what comes next? If you live regretting past decisions you will have much more to regret in the future. Let it go.

Secret:
Perseverance Is The Key to Success

If there are any guarantees in life, one of them is that you will get knocked down. At times like that it's good to remember Vince Lombardi's words, "It's not whether you get knocked down, it's whether you get up."

What we often forget is that even winners lose a lot. Those who are successful are successful because they persevere through pain, suffering, disappointment, humiliation, and more. Being successful is learning to sacrifice to get the things you really want. If you get knocked down, get up, dust yourself off and go forward. Just keep trying!

The movie *Miracle* depicts the amazing story of Herb Brooks, who coached the 1980 U.S. men's Olympic hockey team to a gold medal. But Brooks also knew bitter disappointment earlier in his life. Brooks was the last player to be cut from the 1960 Olympic team, and he sat at home and watched as his teammates went on to win the gold medal that year. Though he made the Olympic teams in 1964 and 1968, the U.S. team did not win medals in either of those games.

Following Brooks' successful college coaching career for the University of Minnesota, he was named coach of the U.S. hockey team before the 1980 Olympics. He took over a team that had the seemingly impossible job of challenging the Soviet team, which under the Olympic Committee rules at the time, allowed top professional teams from communist countries to compete against amateurs from democratic countries. Earlier in the year, the Soviet team had defeated the NHL all-stars 6–0. It was a win that showed they were not only the best hockey team in the world but that they were in a league of their own. Brooks took a bunch of college kids, and through will power and perseverance was able to lead them to win the gold medal by defeating the Soviet team. It might have taken Brooks twenty years, it might have taken a switch from playing to coaching, and it might have taken beating the longest of odds, but he did it. That is perseverance!

For some, many doors will open and their success is dependent upon maximizing their opportunities. For others, few doors will open and they have to go through life with fewer opportunities. For this group, I offer no pity, instead I suggest they get some wood, nails, and a hammer, and build a door. If conventional opportunity doesn't present itself, make your own door and go through it to find your success. In the end, success depends on perseverance.

Many know that Michael Jordan is considered to be one of the great winners in pro basketball history. Not as many people know that in college, Jordan took the shot in the National Championship game to determine if the University of North Carolina would become National Champions. He took the shot and he made it! However, many do not know that during his career Michael Jordan missed the game winning shot twenty-three times. He was a winner because he kept trying.

Greg Jarque, a former student of mine with a larger than life personality, wrote me in an e-mail: "Destiny is something you cultivate, not sit around for."

Keep trying! Just remember that when you get knocked down, get up. If you do that, your successes will far outweigh your failures.

Secret:
Life Is What You Focus On

If you want to change your life, change your focus. It doesn't cost anything and can be accomplished immediately. The completeness of the change is completely up to the person making the change. Remember that whatever we think about is what we are focusing on; we are creating our own reality. Focus is something that we choose. We can focus on the compliment we recently received, on our wonderful children, beautiful music, exciting sports, or the problems of our life. Many people spend much of their life focusing on the negatives in a world of positive and negative choices. We tend to quickly dismiss the good and focus on our troubles. We think about our troubles and obsess.

In 1991 the CW Post Campus of Long Island University named me the first teacher to receive their award as the Outstanding Teacher in Nassau County, New York. As I received the award, I focused on whether or not I really deserved the award. I thought to myself that I don't even know if I'm the best teacher in my department, never mind in all of Nassau County. But as the years went by, I realize that though there were people I worked with who had particular talents that I did not, it did not diminish the things that I did well. I should have focused on the difference that I had made in the lives of young people. I stole some of my own joy the day I received my award by how I focused myself.

Focus is something that each person chooses. A person must look inside themselves whenever they see themselves continually focusing on negative thoughts and determine why it is happening. The best way to prevent it in the future is to determine why it worked for you. Yes, *why it worked for you*. We don't do things willingly unless those things somehow work for us. The reality is that negative focus is like a drug—you get an initial rush of anger, desperation, a sort of negative vibrancy that seems to justify your existence. But, like a drug, the long-term effect of negative focus is the devastation of your life.

We need to deal with why our thoughts often focus on the negative and why so many people do it. We need to consider how to focus on the positive and deal with the negative. We must always remember to find our way back to the positive. If you find yourself in a garden, you can dwell on the beauty of the roses or on the fear of the thorns; it is your choice. But if you choose to have your thoughts consumed with the thorns, you will remember that gardens also attract bees. There will never be an end to the things to worry about if that's your chosen course.

Life isn't about what happens to us, it is about what we do with the circumstances. Most of us can recall witnessing two different people, both in the same bad situation in which a reasonable person would feel beaten, but seeing the two people take very different approaches to handling the situation. One feels the pain but goes forward; the other succumbs to the wound. Individuals who handle misfortune better than others trust at the core level that there is a reason the soul is going through the experience.

You can shape your life much more than you might expect. In fact, in life you pretty much get what you think you deserve. Many people have heard the quote attributed to Abraham Lincoln that says most people are about as happy as they make up their minds to be. And Henry Ford said, "Whether you think you can do it or you think you can't, you are right." If you believe the world is basically bad, it is; if you believe the world is basically good, it is.

Secret:
Tough Times Are Only a Temporary Condition

Many thoughts might help us get through tough times, but one that we rarely consider is that what is, isn't for all time. On July 15, 1992, I lost a son and had another who was so critically ill that doctors told me he would not live through the day—this was occurring as my wife was fighting for her life. July 15th, 1992, was as bad a day as it sounds. But today my wife and I celebrate July 15th as our son revels in his birthday each year. We have parties and reflect on our good fortune and on our miracle son. What is isn't for all time. Sometimes the terrible becomes the wonderful. It is tough to remember that all things are temporary as we go through the bad times, but all things are temporary.

As a young man, Teddy Roosevelt was called home from his office at the New York State Assembly when both his mother and first wife fell ill. He returned home only to lose both his wife and his mother within hours on the same day in the same house. He thought the light had passed from his life forever. He persevered and went on to change the world, find his joy, and raise the daughter who was born only two days earlier.

Upon being hired as the new New York Yankees manager in 1996, Joe Torre had gone through more games in uniform without appearing in a World Series than any man in history. The reports about Joe Torre following his hiring as the Yankee manager were nothing short of embarrassing. He was dubbed "Clueless Joe" by one popular New York newspaper. The radio talk shows practically tore him apart on air as "the wrong man for the job." In fact, virtually no one in New York endorsed his hiring. As many of us now know, his first year as Yankees manager, he took the team to the World Series, and went on to win four Series championships during his first five years as the team's manager. In total, the Yankees went to the playoffs twelve straight years under the direction of a man who had once been dubbed "Clueless Joe" by the media.

When your job is driving you crazy or you find yourself in a situation in which there is not enough money to go around, remind yourself that everything is temporary. It will help. It can also help to remember to value the good times. Your children will grow up, your career will progress and your accomplishments fade into memory, friends you knew as a child will eventually pass on. It is important that we value the moments of life when they happen because they are fleeting. Life was never meant to dwell at one point—it moves constantly. What is today will change tomorrow. Even our talents and bodies are temporary, so try agonizing less about problems and savor the great moments more.

Secret:
Feeling Insecure Is Part of Being Human

Even very secure people are somewhat insecure in social settings. We all want to feel comfortable. The more social the setting, the greater our need to feel secure. Human behavior is fairly consistent and this fact can be used to prepare for feeling more comfortable. If you don't think people are predictable, watch how many people congregate in the kitchen at the next party you attend. People rarely consider the kitchen to be their social entertainment center, but at a get-together it is frequently where people will congregate. There is something in our social fabric that makes kitchens comfort zones, in settings where we might otherwise feel socially awkward.

Practice the art of observing life as you seek your comfort zones. There are places where people just feel comfortable when things are not going well. For many children it is in the loving arms of a parent. For adults it is different for each individual. If you're dealing with difficulties, a comfort zone can be hard to find. The insecurity is brought on by fear of rejection and humiliation. We all want to be accepted and social settings bring out the fear of not being accepted. There are two strategies for going into these situations successfully: First, we can become good actors and pretend nothing fazes us as we project quiet confidence, which can in itself help us relax. The other strategy is to recognize the whole world is insecure so it is better to work on becoming quietly confident in oneself. Try and picture yourself at an event in which everything goes wrong. Recognize that the upshot is you will be fine anyway. Just remember that you are a special person regardless of whether others recognize it or not. The only thing that is important is that you recognize it. And always try to keep your cool!

Secret:
Not Accepting Responsibility Has Become a Way of Life

Isn't it interesting that in this time and era, no one takes responsibility for much of anything? It is always the system, the company, the government or the others who are responsible. Unless of course something has a good outcome, then everyone suddenly claims they are responsible. Success has many fathers, failure is an orphan. A lot of damage to people has been hidden behind the tag, "I'm not responsible," as Nazi war criminals used it at the Nuremberg Trials, and today in America corporate executives cited for the economic collapse. When FBI field agents suspected something was up prior to 9/11, their superiors failed to move forward with investigations of domestic flight schools. After 9/11 and the revelations of such inaction, no one has been held responsible, no one lost their job, and no one was demoted.

When I was teaching, during the first class of the year, I used to point out to students that I never give a student a grade over 90 but I have given failing grades to many kids. Predictably, my students were not happy with that comment and were perplexed because it stood in opposition to my reputation as a "kid-friendly" teacher. I would then finish the thought and say to them, on the day report cards come out, students with high grades say, I got a 95,'—students with a failing grade say, he failed me. It's an illustration that responsibility for one's fate is tossed away fairly early in life. The consequence of a failure to accept responsibility comes when someone doesn't look to correct his problems because he doesn't think it is his problem.

Our society approaches its problems very much like we do as individuals. For example, parts of our inner cities have become centers for housing a permanent underclass—generation after generation born into poverty, combined with an influx of immigrants who have little economic mobility. Out of the inner cities have come children who focus more on survival than on excelling in school. Politicians have failed miserably to deal with this difficult issue, but they still hold the schools accountable for turning around the lives of children that they themselves have failed to help. This is a classic example of failed leadership: if we have a problem, make someone else do something about it. Because of the way our society approaches problems, the problems we have, have become chronic. Solving societal problems is possible, but it takes resolve, perseverance, and patience.

Recovery from the problems that plague today's world begins with individuals taking responsibility. Perhaps the next generation will be better at accepting responsibility. This one clearly has not mastered the concept.

Secret:
You Have to Play the Hand You're Dealt

We are often perplexed and angry at the injustices of life. Some people seem to go through life smoothly while others seem to have to deal with tragedy or a seemingly unending line of difficult experiences. It is a simple fact that we are not all dealt the same hand. Each lifetime has a series of events designed for our soul to experience and grow, and no two souls are here to learn the exact same thing. Some lives will always seem to be incredibly painful and some incredibly easy.

It is important to remember that few lives are as easy as they may look to others. We all have our problems and should remember that a splinter hurts, no matter who gets it stuck in their finger. However, we do have a choice about how to deal with the bad things that happen. We can complain, whine, or wish that our problems would go away. But ultimately it comes down to playing the hand you're dealt. Do the best you can. There are miraculous stories of people who have been dealt an impossible hand and have done great things. Of course, there are also many who have been dealt great hands and parlayed it into nothing.

If you compare yourself and your life to others, most likely nothing good will come of it. Sooner or later, you will come across someone you feel got a better deal than you did. To the best of your ability, look at your life experience on its own merit. At the same time, strive to understand that the painful lessons are helping your soul to mature. The concept of soul maturity admittedly doesn't offer much comfort when you are going through rough times, so perhaps this is the time that you need to trust in God more than other times. In short, bad times happen more to some than others because that is the way it is supposed to be for each soul to achieve its purpose.

You play the hand you're dealt. Play it well and play it with cautious optimism. But if you want to know why God has created such different life experiences on Earth for all of us, the answer is simple: because he left it up to us.

Secret:
We Need a Self-Evaluation from Time to Time to Correct the Course We Are On

It is important to stop and do a self-evaluation from time to time to see if you are really living the values you believe in. In other words, learn to understand if your actions are true to you. For example, if asked which is more enjoyable, work or family time, most people would place time with their family ahead of time at work. But, are they really finding joy in family life? Often, people who do not spend a great deal of time with their family are doing so because they are not getting the same positive feelings from family that they get from their accomplishments at work. At work, one may be deemed important by others and the somewhat simpler responsibilities of home life may seem mundane in comparison. Learn to understand why you do what you do. Balance is achieved by understanding oneself.

The first thing we all need to do is meet survival needs, and that can mean more hours at work than we would like or would have chosen in life. However, often it is a choice to spend time away from our family—and we must make our choices from love and not from fear. For example, we often live out of alignment because we fear not having enough or being enough. As we consider our lives, we must consider what is real and what is a creation of our fear.

As mentioned earlier, values are the equivalent of software that runs our brain. In our self-evaluation it is important to determine how many of our values are derived from fear and how many from love. Ask yourself; is your life in alignment with your own values? As is often noted, at the end of our lives, no one wishes they had spent more time at the office.

Secret:
Take Time to Consider All the Things You Have Done Right With Your Life

For most people, reflection about our past is dominated by decisions we consider to have been mistakes, or events in which we believe someone has done us wrong. We rarely sit back and reflect on all our wise choices and good deeds. For many, the pattern of reflection is about beating ourselves up and second-guessing ourselves, asking, why did I choose to work for that company, go to that school, marry that person, etc.? Of course, each of these questions can consume us with regret.

One of the most important lessons we need to learn through our life experience is to love ourselves. Many people are stuck in this phase of development because they are more caught up with their failures than they are with their many successes. Loving oneself is not narcissistic or casting oneself in a mode of being overly self-involved. It is about recognizing our own goodness and connection to the creator and all things.

When we focus on our past mistakes in order to self-correct for the future, we are engaging in a beneficial practice. But most of the time, when we focus on mistakes we have made, we are simply beating ourselves up and reliving unpleasant moments over and over. This is not only a displeasing practice, it takes us further away from recognizing our own worth and engaging in appropriate self-love. We always must remember that our life is what we choose to focus on. Focusing on self-regret is a harmful practice.

We make many choices and decisions every hour each day. The human experience comes fully equipped with regret regarding the roads we choose and don't choose. When we have regrets it is important to let it go and move on with a smile. Yes, if we all had to do it again, we would have made wiser choices, smarter investments, treated others differently and more. So do that—only start today. Use a lifetime of acquired knowledge for wiser choices, smarter investments and to treat others differently.

Most importantly, when we play the reflection game, remember to dwell on all the good things we have done, all the good fortune that has come our way, and all the things that we are grateful for. Reflect on the little things we have done to make the lives of others better. And most of all, remember when we think of our lives in retrospect—take a breath, look in the mirror and smile at a job well done.

Secret:
Controlling One's Emotions and Anger
Are Crucial to a Balanced Life

Simply put, a balanced life and good decision making is intertwined with the ability to control one's emotions.

Some people are very reactive and we brand their behavior with a number of uncomplimentary names. Emotions are the domain of the reptilian part of our brain. When the reptilian portion of the brain goes unchecked we can expect tantrums, hotheaded reactions and more. Our usual way of dealing with people who are quick to anger is to tell them to get a grip or get under control. Sometimes individuals are capable of doing that upon verbal directive.

The contrasting personality is the individual who seems to approach life in a steady and even manner. These are people who have their emotions under control. There is a reason that certain individuals go through life in a state of calm. These people have allowed wisdom to rule their emotions. These individuals have learned not to live life with the highest highs and the lowest lows. They are not going to be the one who gets angry when their rental car is not ready or their plane is delayed. They are not going to get angry when there is another way to approach a situation.

At times, we show special respect to the angry because they are the more likely to take on the powerful and we admire that. But Gandhi and Christ took on the powerful and they used love as their message. It would be best to learn from them. Anger is like heroin—it feels great at first and steals your life in the end; in between you're a mess. It is important to remember that frustrations should not and cannot be ignored. Frustrated people need to deal with their feelings in an appropriate manner or their frustrations become anger. Short-circuit the anger by dealing with the frustration that often breeds the disease. When circumstances breed frustrations, just ask the question that got inspirational

speaker and author Alan Cohen to focus on what's really important: "What if this were all alright?" When you feel the frustration
mounting, stop for a moment to think: What if this is one of the
tests God chose for you based on the decisions you have made?
Would you still be frustrated and angry?

Short-circuiting anger takes continuing effort to master. It can
be very hard to look at life in a calm and deliberate manner and
still remain passionate about our world. We often confuse a calm
and deliberate manner with the passionless and detached. With
practice, you can come to accept what is and still be passionate
and driven in the game of life. It is all right to be driven to achieve
important goals in life; we just don't want the drive to use our
health and happiness as its fuel. Angry people tend to do just that
and sacrifice their health and happiness in pursuit of sometimes
elusive or unattainable goals. Anger is self-destructive and hurts
everyone around us.

If anger is so bad for us, and we know it, why do so many of
us walk around angry? The reason so many people choose to be
constantly angry is they have learned to feed off the chemicals
released in the body that accompany the emotion. Anger gives
us a biochemical rush, with lots of stimulating stuff, among them
adrenaline. We can feel alive in our anger. It is difficult to let go of
anger because anger makes you feel empowered. The problem is
that it will ruin your life if you don't get it under control.

Anger is also usually accompanied by feelings that our anger
is justified. There is a mechanism that self-validates the state of
anger in the human mind. So an angry person can feel better at
first, feeling justified in their actions, which often allows them to
initiate actions that they might not attempt if they weren't angry.
Anger is a human drug that makes your body feel good at first, but
you become sick and desperate as time goes by.

Everything within the reasonable range is fine. As human
beings we respond to an insult or slight from another with a heated
defense. We are creatures with great wisdom and great emotion.

The emotions help us to live a richer life. When they get out of control it is similar to putting too much spice or seasoning on food. Just the right amount makes the food heavenly, too much renders it unpalatatable. And so it is with emotions and life. Without emotions, life is just plain dull and we can lack passion and drive; too much emotion and life gets too hot to handle.

Wisdom is the measuring spoon for our emotions. Be wise enough to put life's problems in perspective. If you cannot control your emotions, frustration can become anger, which sours a person from the inside out. It steals your smile, joy, and eventually your life. What would happen if you stopped being angry, fighting what is, stopped complaining and wishing that what is never happened? Perhaps, you would be on the way to what you most desire at this moment, happiness on Earth. Don't worry about how to gain wisdom. Trust yourself, you know what is right and what is wrong. Feelings of love, hate, envy, fear and injustice, can lead to an unleashing of unchecked emotions. It is important to always work to keep your emotions in balance.

If a person truly believes in the creator, consider that in your everyday life, the plan is for you to pursue justice, equality, fraternity, and even love. Anger doesn't make it happen, it prevents it from happening.

Secret:
The Human Brain Can Be Reprogrammed

The brain is a great tool. Unfortunately it does not come with a user's manual. Its hardware allows us to recover from frequent abuse and poor programming as we indoctrinate the brain with conflicting data, often harmful to our health. What runs our brain is software that we program as we are socialized to our culture throughout our lifetime.

Much of the culture we have programmed into our brain is conflict free, and therefore, the brain accepts that data well. For example, there is not a legitimate organization or group in Western culture that accepts cannibalism. So the brain clearly programs itself with a message that the practice is abhorrent to everything that is good and right. On the other hand, we are told not to abuse alcohol and drugs. We are told this in our homes, churches, by our political leaders, and other social institutions. However, older peers, movies, and songs tell us differently. This is where the software in the brain gets conflicting messages and problems arise. This is also an indication of how the human brain is better than computers. It is equipped to sift through conflicting data, although it does get led astray.

We should not assume that the software the brain acquires in life is permanent. Software can be rewritten, and therefore, so can the program running your brain. A change in your behavior will come about if you change your programming. Change the message in the brain, and you will change your approach to the things that are determining your life. Many things like drugs and alcohol have a physiological component that makes changing behavior more difficult. But all things being equal, the brain is a powerful force. I wouldn't bet against it if the new software is powerful enough.

We must remember that the brain receives messages in the form of natural chemicals secreted in the body. Introducing powerful agents from outside the body's own biochemical system like drugs or alcohol, affects the brain by changing the chemical message. This could have a devastating effect on life if not handled reasonably. The brain will change structurally when exposed to enough of these outside chemicals.

Just think of the brain like a new electronic device you have recently purchased that came without a manual. You are unlikely to send it back, but you are going to experiment with it to see what it can do. But just like with the new electronic toy, computer, or television we have purchased, we are unlikely to take the time to figure out how to master the product. Whatever your values are— to be happy, to contribute to the world through your work, to enjoy your family, to find time for your favorite hobbies—you need to program the brain to the task selected. Like everything that is in our control, the choice is ours. Not learning how to work all the functions on the TV remote is one thing; in the case of the brain, it will have a compromising effect on life if you don't take the time to learn.

Secret:
Make Important Decisions When You Are at Your Best

Avoid making decisions when you are tired. Avoid confronting people when you are tired. These might sound like simple rules, but virtually everything looks worse and we make poorer choices when we are fatigued. If you want evidence, the techniques for breaking people who are captured as terrorists include sleep deprivation. Terroristic regimes have long used the tactic of arresting their enemies in the middle of the night when the person will be most surprised and disoriented. So why would you make crucial decisions when you are in a state of fatigue?

We often make crucial decisions by wearing ourselves down until we can't think anymore. Then we often take the action that someone else wants us to take or one that seems the easiest road to take because we have worn ourselves out. The best time to make important decisions is to be well rested and then align your decisions with your own goals for life. Does the decision take you closer to your life plan or further away? You can even make a list of pros and cons. Just be sure that your fears don't overcome your desire to seek out a meaningful life.

When we are confused about what the right decision is—and we so often face this situation—it is always best to reconnect to the soul's basic message. Make decisions from a loving and understanding state of mind.

Secret:
We Can Summarize What it Takes to Be Happy

Life can improve immediately once we recognize that we all have
a right to live our lives happily and joyfully. Life can and should
be fun. Too many of us are caught in a revolving cycle of failing
life strategies that doesn't work for us. For many, lack of joy results
from their own core beliefs and values. Despite the fact that many
of us have fairly comfortable lives, so many people still find much
to be unhappy about and complain.

When we understand and accept that human life supplies us
with a never-ending list of things that *we think* we need, we can
better deal with the fact that if we base happiness on the satisfac-
tion of our chosen needs, we will never be happy. The problem
is that most of us have not recognized that we don't have to be
unhappy and that human needs are often not real needs, but are
lifestyle choices. When we fail to satisfy this need, instead of revis-
iting whether it is real or not, we become unhappy. Unhappiness
comes from not getting or achieving what we decided we needed
to get or achieve to be happy. In these cases we often focus our
thoughts on fear, or specifically on things in our past that we perceived as unfair, and we combine them with how we think about
our present situation.

Happiness and joy can be increased with the knowledge that
the central trait among people who are happy is that they like
themselves. So of course it would be natural to ask what the secret
to liking oneself is. Let's begin with asking the question, "Are you
a good person?" Invariably, we respond to an inquiry about being
a good person in terms of others. For example, we might answer,
"Yes, I am a good person because I am kind to others, generous to
my community, care for my children, and never hurt anyone on
purpose." This shows more than an answer to a simple question; it
is a road map to liking ourselves and therefore becoming happier.
The more you think of others, the happier you are; the more you
think of yourself, the less happy you will be.

Liking oneself as a result of service to others is one key to happiness. The other key to happiness can be found in another piece of wisdom from Abraham Maslow, the psychologist who is known for creating *Maslow's Hierarchy of Needs*. It is Maslow's viewpoint that the only people who are truly happy are people involved in work they find meaningful. Most of us do not consider work as crucial to happiness, but work is crucial to leading a happy life. Also remember that our work is how we achieve the resources we need to survive. Therefore, if your job isn't meaningful beyond meeting your survival needs, you can always look to service to your community and to your neighbors. Many people have found their greatest rewards in working outside their job.

Happiness comes from the ability to see oneself as a good and valuable person. In other words, to like oneself we must believe that we are making a contribution to others. Dan Baker, a psychologist who studies happiness extensively describes in his book *What Happy People Know,* how he counseled one of his patients to find happiness by working as an assistant in a cancer ward. The man, wealthy and successful, subsequently helped a cashier in a 7-Eleven whose mother was suffering from cancer. He finds his worth, happiness, and smile by helping others and making his spare time meaningful. Ladies and gentlemen, it begins with that, and it ends wherever you take it.

Motivational speaker Anthony Robbins points out that we all live our lives seeking happiness and attempting to avoid pain. The funny thing about life is that our materialistic society often takes us in the opposite direction of happiness. There is nothing wrong with working hard doing something you enjoy and making money while doing it. The problem is brought on by a tendency of human nature—when one focuses solely on career success and making money. These individuals are lucky if they have time for family; seldom do they have time for selfless acts of kindness. Often in life the focus of meeting our needs becomes all encompassing. The result is an unhappy person who is missing the important components in the equation of happiness.

When we consider that happiness comes from liking oneself and believing that one is a good person, we can begin to understand how a person who lived in poverty, took a vow of celibacy, and lived among the poorest of the poor, could be a content and happy person. Looking at Mother Theresa's life clarifies a lot of things for us. She was not only a role model for human kindness; she was a role model for human happiness.

2. Energy, Reincarnation, and Relationships

Secret:
Everything Is Energy

It is hard to think of our tangible, touchable world as anything but solid. But the truth is everything is energy. If you look at your hand under the right kind of microscope you would see the movement of energy. Human beings are energy that vibrates very slowly to allow for a physical experience. The interesting thing is that our physical body, which we consider to be what we are, is a carrying case that we need to treasure and protect. But in the long run we are energy, not the physical body we will one day leave behind in the same way that a caterpillar leaves its casing as it becomes a butterfly.

Energy exists on different vibration levels. When energy vibrates at its slowest—it appears solid. So as we look at our hand, the chair we are sitting on, or our home, we would swear that it is solid. And for all intents and purposes, for the time being, each is solid.

In the introduction to "Part I: Secrets of Death" I discussed the different states of water. H_2O can be vapor, water, or ice depending on the temperature. What temperature does is slow down or speed up the vibrations of the water molecules, and at certain temperatures water transitions from one state to another. When we leave this world, we leave our body behind as a shell or carrying case for the soul that has outlived its usefulness. That is when our spiritual side begins to vibrate faster, leaves the body, and it returns to the other side.

Before that day comes and during our life on Earth, the energy in us has, in effect, two modes of vibration. Internally, we are comprised of two different governing forces. The psychic Edgar Cayce called the two decision-making forces within us the *personality* and the *individuality*. Individuality is spiritually acquired, and it is the part of us that knows of the other side and has knowledge of our many previous lives. Individuality is the keeper of the soul's mission, the part that knows why we came to Earth and what we desire to experience and learn as we affect the world in a positive way. Personality is earth-acquired and only sees the world in the here and now. It only concerns itself with the visible and tangible elements of the world.

As we live our lives on Earth, it is important that an appropriate balance exists between individuality and personality. Too much individuality and we will not have a full life experience; too much personality and we separate our self from God and start making decisions based on the shallow considerations of earthly human experience. Acts of evil are created by personality-driven entities because fear is a major factor in suppressing individuality. The more a life becomes driven by personality, the more it suppresses individuality and the more it loses the balance necessary for learning the lessons our soul came to Earth to learn.

An example of a personality-driven action is the hatred of others based on socialized values. For example, the Nazis used hatred of Jews as a vehicle for blaming Germany's failures on an internal enemy. A child raised by members of the Nazi party was brought up with values based on a hatred of innocent people. The individuality in a person knows that all people are from the same creator and that the central unifying force of the universe is love. So when a person acted with love for all humankind in a society such as that in Germany before and during World War II, it was the individuality in that person that had filtered the earthly personality-driven "wrong message."

Put another way, we can think of these counterbalancing forces in us as soul energy, driven by individuality, and earth energy, which comes from personality. The more the entity becomes driven by earth energy, the more it suppresses the soul energy. Soul energy is crucial for a balanced and successful experience on Earth. So a person whose soul energy is suppressed tries to make up for the missing energy by accessing the *earth energy* of others. Feelings are an emotional form of earth energy. In affecting another entity by creating bad feelings, the personality-driven entity feels a sense of control and feels it gains the energy that it lacks. Note that what is really lacking is the *soul energy* that was suppressed in the first place. The *earth energy* gained doesn't truly fill the void, so the feeling of control never satisfies.

When the personality dominates our lives, we suppress that which we are supposed to do (focus on what we have come to Earth to learn) and instead accept a false agenda created in this incarnation. A personality-driven soul eats up energy and causes a soul to feel depleted. As such, the personality-driven soul is always on the hunt for an energy boost. It gets the energy boost from tapping into the energy of others. As such, evil actions derive from personality-driven entities and their need for energy.

It is always about energy, and everything in the universe is energy. We are two forces in one, but we are healthiest when they act in concert with each other. Individuals brought up in a loving, caring environment and taught to love and respect others are living with the two sides acting in concert—the energy in balance. What results is a wonderful, productive life and a person who is a joy to know.

Secret:
Reincarnation Helps Our Soul to Progress

Have you ever gone into a room and spotted a person that you know you are really going to like? And when you meet them, your pre-cognition is true. Or the opposite happens and you meet a person that you know you are going to dislike? The most obvious cause is that you have recognized their soul from a prior life. The research on reincarnation comes from multiple sources. Most notably, Dr. Ian Stevenson a psychiatrist who did his research at the University of Virginia, Edgar Cayce, Dr. Brian Weiss, and Dr. Raymond Moody all contribute remarkably to form a more complete picture of reincarnation.

Dr. Stevenson researched young children who spoke about their prior lives in such authentic detail that it led those around them to research the story. Remarkably, numerous cases revealed that the child was providing information about the prior life that they had absolutely no way of knowing about unless they were in fact the reincarnated soul. Dr. Stevenson concluded that his studies provided ample room for a rational person, if he wants, to believe in reincarnation on the basis of evidence.

Dr. Brian Weiss, a medically trained psychotherapist, uses hypnosis to regress souls into prior lives. The remarkable thing is that under hypnosis, the person frequently recognizes people in their past life as people who exist in their present life. However, the individuals have frequently switched roles: A beloved sister may now be an aunt; a best friend in a prior life may be your brother in this life; and so on.

Edgar Cayce, when he was in a psychic trance, frequently pointed out relationships from a past life were affecting relationships in this life. For example, he told a woman who complained about treatment she was receiving from her sister: "Well, it is understandable why your sister is treating you this way. In your last life you stole her husband."

Dr. Raymond Moody's main work dealt with the study of people who died and returned to their body within minutes. This hardly would constitute reincarnation. However, one of the people who returned to life following a suicide attempt told this story: She reported that she was given a choice to stay on the other side or return back to her body. But she was told that if she did not go back she would have to have the same experiences up to this point in her next life, so that she will learn to make a different choice— clearly an indication of the existence of karmic debt.

We are reincarnated until our soul has progressed to the point in which it has mastered the lessons that Earth can provide. At that point, the soul can either work on progression through the various levels of heaven or return as an aide to those on Earth. Most of us are in various progressions of reincarnation; learning lessons and moving forward. This is the natural order of things on Earth.

Secret:
Learn to Deal with Paradox and Conflict Through Balance

Life and relationships are confusing because a successful life demands embracing contrasting values and actions. Life and relationships are paradoxical, and sometimes full of conflict. In fact, life is a paradox. Learn to deal with it. And life features conflict. Get used to it.

We need to understand that life has us embrace paradoxical values. We need to be kind yet we need to be tough. We need to listen to others yet we need to trust our own instincts. We need to work hard yet we must enjoy life. We must trust our own hearts in worshiping God yet we must respect the views of others. We are always required to be both hard and soft, both kind and demanding, and so on. The answer to dealing with this paradox is *balance.* Not too much and not too little is the way to forge a successful life. Remember to emphasize the things that are important to you. Having a happy family life and also achieving career success is possible, as long as you remember to live in balance.

As for conflict, another form of balance is called for. There is the old axiom that walking down the middle of the road doubles your chances of getting hit by a car. One should not seek conflict, but when we try to avoid it we normally find ourselves in a more difficult position. Learn to manage it, since it is inevitable. Here, balance is like moderation. Begin with a simple rule like not using hurtful words when dealing with conflict. Hurtful words move a conflict into a new dimension, obviously not a good one. It is important to determine what we want from the other person. If you intend to hurt them, it is not a conflict, it is just using words to be mean-spirited. In conflict, we are attempting to convince someone that we are right on a particular issue. This can only occur if you leave room for the other person to move to your position. If you put others in a corner, they will come out fighting.

But disputes should not be about proving you are right and others are wrong. That is simple ego gratification. Be sure to establish from the beginning of a conflict that intelligent people not only can have different opinions about an issue but frequently do. Convincing the other side that you are right may never happen since the root of the conflict may be based on differing perceptions and subjective views of an issue. If you cannot convince a person to see your side of an issue and move closer to it, a more reasonable goal is to admit that although you may not agree, you respect them and their opinion. Try and work with other people if you can, but it may not always be possible. Some people just are not going to like you precisely because of the things you believe in. Get over it. It is part of life.

Paradox may look more peaceful on the outside, but it is like a conflict from within. When the brain is given contrasting values it has a difficult time. The state of mind when we attempt to hold two thoughts of contrasting values is called cognitive dissonance. When that happens we find we must rationalize one of the values to make our thoughts mutually compatible. The truth is, often a paradox is better dealt with by balance and not rationalization. There is nothing confusing about doing the right thing. Live in balance and life will take its proper course.

Secret:
People Are Always Going to Be Difficult; Learn Forgiveness and Patience

When Groucho Marx was into his eighth decade on Earth he was asked in an interview about the secret of a long life. He replied, "Have a lot of friends." The interviewer followed with the question, "What is the secret to having a lot of friends?" Groucho replied, "Have a short memory." Groucho had learned through a lifetime of experience what we all need to learn—that people who are our friends will disappoint us from time to time and we must learn to forgive them. People will give you more than enough reasons to discontinue a friendship: Know them long enough and they will have wronged you or disappointed you or simply not lived up to your expectations. If the person's good qualities outweigh their bad ones, let go of your anger and disappointment. You will be richer for the ability to forgive.

By no means am I advocating that we should dismiss or ignore all the negative activities or hurtful actions of others. As we all come to learn at some point, there truly are some people who you should not have in your life. You are better off without them. People are paradoxical; they are both simple and complicated. Relationships are often difficult because people are not always consistent in their behavior. Frequently someone's reaction to an event or to a statement is based on something occurring in their life that is unknown to you and not on the particular interaction of the moment. We often misinterpret such actions and may ascribe a motive for them that really wasn't intended to be. When such things happen, it is important to remember that relationships are situational. What can be a very good friendship in one set of circumstances can be a very difficult encounter in another. For example, you may have a wonderful relationship with your stock broker when the market is on an upswing and making lots of money. When forces out of your brokers control occur and the market goes down, inevitably you may see him as a diminished character in your life.

The important question is whether the person is a good person and whether they will be there for you when you need them. You may have friends who are fun but in times of need you find them missing in action. That is OK as long as you can differentiate the expectations you have of different friends. If you can't, then you will have a difficult time beings friends with the people I call "charismatic nonsupporters." Before you dismiss a person and choose to exclude them from your life because of an action you find objectionable, you need to examine if your life would be better or worse if that person were no longer part of your day-to-day experience.

The answer to dealing with difficult people is to forgive them and love them anyway. It might help to consider that virtually all of us are difficult and self-centered at moments of our lives. If we understand why people do what they do, in many cases, we can forgive them for their actions and keep them in our lives, and ultimately as part of our life experience.

Secret:
We Can Separate Ourselves from Damaging People and Energy Thieves

When it comes to dealing with people who cause damage to others, we need to learn to recognize them for what they are and forgive them. But that does not mean it is a good idea to have this type of person around in your life. It is absolutely true that forgiveness is an incredible resource in creating a happy life. We should surround ourselves with good friends, even if they have made a mistake or two in the past. Good people who make mistakes are very different from people who consistently and constantly bring hurt into our lives. Individuals who are damaged may actually be energy thieves who steal energy from healthy people. They are, in effect, parasites.

Energy thieves are people who have a soul that has receded into their body and therefore lack the energy necessary for life. These individuals must steal energy, and healthy people are their targets. There are numerous reasons for why their soul may have receded into the body (the most common is suffering a great trauma at a young age), but the reason why they have become energy thieves is not as important to you as the harm you need to avoid. Unless handled appropriately, the energy thief will leave you worse off after an encounter. If there is someone who is part of your everyday life who constantly steals your energy, you need to consider changing the relationship. You can encounter energy thieves in the workplace, in the family, among your friends—basically in every kind of encounter in life. Many "crazy bosses" are energy thieves. The soul in need of energy seeks positions in which it can exploit other people.

It may not always be possible to simply pull yourself away from an energy thief. If you care about the person, for example, you may want to help them rehabilitate. You will need to suggest somehow that they find their soul, though be aware that self-reflection is unlikely for an energy thief since they tend not to recognize what has happened to them. Remember that problems are only solved when the energy thief is willing to recognize their issues, and that is fairly unlikely. If you can't change them, you need to create rules they must follow to continue in the relationship with you. Failing that, you need to separate yourself from them.

It is interesting that this character trait in the workplace is often found among those in positions of authority. This type of individual can be successful because they will pay any price and do anything for advancement, and frequently the process of advancement in business or educational administration facilitates soul recession. Bad bosses get themselves into positions of authority over others so they can steal their energy. It is terrible to be working for this type of person. Our own personal situations may not always provide us the flexibility to get away from these types of characters when we encounter them in the workplace. Therefore, people have to find a way to survive under less than ideal conditions. The human spirit is terrific. It survived concentration camps, and it can survive energy thieves. If you are in this type of situation you must set rules wherever you can about how you are treated. Without rules to control their behavior, there will be health consequences for you as well as effects on your happiness. But don't leave it at that; plan for a way to move out of the situation. Also, be aware that many energy thieves take on the role of "professional victim". For them, the game is about getting your energy, and playing the role of victim can be quite effective in helping them get what they want.

People whose soul has regressed are not evil, they are lost. They do bad things because the soul has retreated into the body to protect itself from being hurt. They are people whose soul has gone so deep into the body, that sometimes you can no longer recognize there is a soul present. Healthy souls, wanting to do good, frequently look for the antidote to give to people whose souls have regressed. However, reclaiming the soul is not very easy. For the person involved, recognizing that the soul needs to be reclaimed is hard since this is the person's natural state. Though they are capable of doing very bad things, they still have parents, friends, wives and husbands and others who care about them. They rarely recognize their behavior as wrong even when others point it out. The best opening for change is recognizing that the source of the problem can sometimes be traced to a difficult time in early life. Sometimes they can be approached and helped on a selfish level. The problem is convincing them that they would be happier by changing. The story of Scrooge is a classic example of a recessed soul that was unaware that it was in that condition. Hopefully, others can change without the visit of three ghosts.

If you choose to take on the task of helping a recessed soul, it will not be easy. This type of person tries to avoid having truthful people around who are capable of confronting them with the truth. It is their defense mechanism. But if you can find the good in the person, then the soul hasn't recessed so far that it isn't reachable.

Dealing with a person so they can realize they are living with a recessed soul is likely to lead to a confrontation. However, it is crucial that any confrontation be designed around love, and not on hurting the individual, even though they have hurt others. The best chance for success lies in illustrating for the person how their life is not working. They will be pretty callous about the lives of others because they are in such pain themselves, so it won't be easy. Attempts to help often fail, and have consequences for all involved. Then again, if you are successful, improving a life is worth the work.

Secret:
There Can Be a System Where Everyone Wins

Our entire human system of interactions seems to be based on someone winning and someone losing. Whether we are looking at human relationships through a lens of social interaction, political power, or economic transactions, there always seems to be winners and losers. In fact, some of the sweetness of winning comes from knowing that you are not the poor schnook who lost. We have raised our children to be competitive and when we have problems, we look at competition to be the answer. After all, the capitalist system has made America the richest nation in the world (though I should add, that has not made Americans the happiest people in the world).

In New York State, as well as in many other parts of the country, competitive spirit is being used to improve schools. The concept is that if we identify which schools are losers, we can make everyone work harder. Of course, the accountability system ignores many factors that affect school performance, such as the relationship between spending per pupil and student achievement. The hypothesis is that being put on a failing list will embarrass school officials and that fear will prompt action needed for the schools to improve. And of course the politicians and the officials of the various states' education departments will not have to deal with the real problems of children and schooling. Of course this will not work, schools will only be fixed with a system based on love and not fear.

Many people saw the film *A Beautiful Mind* and learned about, even if they did not fully understand, Nash's theory of governing dynamics, which does not emphasize winning at all costs but making your best choice based on knowing what others are going to do or want in the situation. It is a way of thinking that allows you to win but takes the focus off having a loser. It is as if you were to ask: What if no one lost? What if we can all win?

Try applying that broadly, not just to one situation. What if there was enough for everyone to have the life they want? What if we approached life from that vantage point? What if life was based on a principle in which we all win and we gain no pleasure from watching the defeat of another? In a world like that everyone can continue to do what is best for themselves but also do it without feeling they have to beat everyone who gets in their way.

Obviously, we would need some new rules to live by as well as think of new ways to socialize our children. But a world in which everyone wins is certainly nice to think about. It sounds naïve and unrealistic, but so did the idea of men standing on the moon.

Secret:
Make People Around You Feel Good About Themselves—Give Them Credit and Say You Admire Them

The act of giving a person credit for their good work is a thing of beauty! A colleague who does it is a wonderful person. A boss who does it is a success! Giving credit to others is a very difficult thing for some, but it is a key to achieving your goals. People love being around someone who makes them feel good. Giving credit and praise easily and frequently is a surefire way to build a following of individuals who will work for you now and stay with you in the future. And giving praise doesn't always have to be about a job well done. Tell the person you admire them or how wonderful they are, and tell others. It is likely to get back to the person you are praising that you are telling other people they are special, and they will be eternally grateful for your kind gesture. Additionally, people around you will see you as a person who says positive things about others. Don't hesitate to compliment a person to others in front of the person you are complimenting. On the other hand, if you trash people...well, you know how that turns out.

However, it is important not to be a phony. If you are, any compliments you give will sound hollow, and you will be considered shallow. To practice this philosophy, you really have to find the good in people, which can be hard if it has not been part of your approach to life. But as with all things, finding the good in people gets easier the more you do it. If you are sincere in your praise, it is a beautiful thing.

All this requires learning not to let your own self-interests get in the way of seeing what is good in others. A general rule in life is that keeping your ego in check can lead to success. The problem with ego is articulated in the story of the frog that asks two birds for a ride south for the winter. The frog comes up with a scheme that if the birds can hold a stick between them the frog will hold on and hitch a ride with them as they fly south. When other frogs see the three flying by, they ask in admiration whose idea it was?

The frog can't resist taking credit, so he lets go of the stick to point to himself and falls.

Interestingly, Jim Collins in his book on superior companies, *Good to Great,* notes that outstanding leaders who led companies to greatness tended to be hard-driving when it came to furthering the company's interests but humble as individuals. If you are in a leadership position, recognize the contributions of others. If things are going well it is only because people around you are doing the right thing. Managers get credit for picking the right people and staying out of their way as everyone works toward a common goal.

Additionally, those who have learned the Law of Attraction through writings such as Norman Vincent Peale's *The Power of Positive Thinking* or Rhonda Byrnes's *The Secret* will know, the more people in your life you find worthy of praise—the more praiseworthy people you will attract into your world. Then, whenever possible, tell them how wonderful they are.

It is important to remember that virtually all successful people got to the height of their achievements with the help of others. When you take an honest look at how you became successful, you should see all the people who helped you get there. Remember to thank them!

Secret:
Relationships Are Situational

One of the most surprising factors we deal with as our life progresses is the fact that relationships change based on the times and the situation we are in. Good friends in one phase of life are barely visible in another part of life. People who work closely together to reach a common goal may actually have a completely different relationship with each other after the goal has been met. When you start a new job or find yourself in a new circumstance, you may find that people who once were your close friends may not be in your foremost thoughts.

Of course, there are close relationships that last a lifetime. There are people who are at your side regardless of the life circumstance. These are special relationships that need to be treasured; their value is greater than gold. But in reality, life has designed most relationships to be situational. Friends come and go, colleagues come and go, and we should learn a little from each relationship as we move down the road of life.

We often lose touch with people who have played an important role during a portion of our life. This is the way life has been designed to unfold. Often souls play an important part in our life for a period of time and then disappear from our everyday existence. We need not regret the loss of these important entities as they we will be reunited again when the time is right.

It is often fun to consider the relationship that two souls had in a prior lifetime. We recognize familiar souls when we meet them. Sometimes the past relationship was a good one—sometimes not so good. The important thing is that we have carried forward our feelings and emotions toward that soul into this lifetime. Sometimes our soul desires to thank another for help that was rendered in a past life. Sometimes our soul desires forgiveness from the other and sometimes our soul wants to receive justice from a soul that has hurt us in the past. In these cases, God wants us to discover the grace of forgiveness.

Secret:
Think Before You Speak/Think Before You Marry

The fact that we put up with a great deal of difficulty in our relationships is an indication of how awful loneliness can be. People seem to marry without a great deal of consideration as to the lifelong impact that the choice will have. It is perhaps the most important decision we make in life that many of us make without considering its full implications. A person usually marries the type of people he or she dates. A person will date and marry a person who treats them the way he or she thinks they deserve to be treated. Yes, the key to who we date and marry is based on our own self-image. If a person gets involved in abusive relationships in the dating process, the same will follow in marriage. People who get involved with individuals who treat them badly, and eventually marry someone who treats them badly, are getting what they themselves believe they deserve. The important distinction is, it is not what they deserve, it is what they *think* they deserve. Often, therapy to reclaim one's self-esteem is necessary before beginning a healthy relationship.

When we consider the choices we make in a lifetime, marrying the wrong person can be one of the more painful decisions. The problems of marrying the wrong person become compounded multiple times when children are involved. Souls radiate to other souls; be sure the souls radiating to you are the right ones. Even when you marry the right person, marriage is something you have to work at. Two people, each with their own view of life and their own needs, must merge and find a commonality. As the years pass it is important to be able to adapt to the changes that occur in our spouse. Additionally, it is important to keep a sense of humor and recognize that we all want the ideal and none of us are quite so ideal. My wife and I laugh as I tell her that what she wanted in a husband is a strong man who will do whatever she tells him to do. I suspect that we all want the perfect person that none of us are.

One important secret to a successful marriage and relationship is to avoid hurtful words. Hurtful words may give an advantage in an argument, but they will permanently damage a relationship. Once said, you can't take back the damage, the humiliation, and the hurt you cause. Look at the bigger picture. Lose the argument and win the relationship!

Secret:
Give Your Child a Strong Foundation

One of the toughest things in life is to see your child's disappointment or worse yet, your child's pain. Wise and loving parents plan, strategize, and try to do everything possible to provide wonderful, happy lives for their children. Unfortunately, overprotective parents do not always appreciate that their children, just like all other people on Earth, are here for their souls to experience life. As parents we may want our children to have a perfect life, but that is not why they are here. Just like us, our children are on this Earth to have the soul grow as a result of earthly learning. We can plan for our children to have a perfect life. Just be prepared for the fact that God, and therefore our soul, has a different plan. Still, all parents hope to shape this experience on Earth as one in which pleasant lessons are learned and pain is minimal.

Everything begins with a strong foundation. From the creation of a home or office building to the raising of a child, a broken foundation is a certain predictor of future hardships. In working over three decades with teenagers I have witnessed many parents who have lost their ability to communicate with their own children, parents who lost the ability to direct their child through the minefield of life. They come in many varieties, from those who are in denial to those who come to school officials for answers on what to do. Most of the time these families have the same problem— they did not take the time to build an appropriate foundation with their child when the child was very young. When children are younger their emotional needs cannot be neglected. A parent will surely pay in ever increasing increments for not attending to their child's needs. The bottom line is that to build a foundation it takes time and selfless acts on the part of the parent. The investment in children includes but is not limited to: time, joy, loving re-correction, two-way communication, appropriate role-modeling, and love. As time passed, parents who have not provided an appropriate foundation may find themselves in the principal's office with their child because the child's behavior is either hurtful to others or self-destructive, and frequently both. (Hopefully this meeting happens in the principal's office and not in the police station.) Often, the parent wants the school to find a quick fix. Our modern society has become famous for seeking the quick fix. We want to fix our children the way people in today's society want to fix everything, with quick solutions that do not require a great deal of painful sacrifice. However, quick fixes rarely work in anything in life, and they most certainly never do with children.

The first thing to understand about parenting is that the experience is a two-way street. The child is learning their own way through life with a road map that you are providing. Your role as a parent is one of the reasons why you are on this Earth in the first place. It is part of your life experience. The right answer for parenting is to build the foundation correctly from the beginning. Damage control is never going to provide you with the rock solid structure that you can have had you used the ingredients for a strong foundation in the first place. If you have not built the right foundation and are now suffering the consequences, go back to the beginning and do an inventory of what you did right and what you did wrong. A repaired foundation is better than one that continues to be neglected. If you search your heart and truly listen to your child, you will know what to do next. Be prepared to devote time, love, patience and lots of energy. The payoff to doing the right thing is a child who will be the light of your life. And as much as you do in your career and community, it will not compare with the impact you will have on the future by raising a righteous person.

From time to time, don't forget to tell your children how special you think they are. They will give you back the "You're supposed to think I'm wonderful—you're my Mom/Dad," line. It doesn't matter that they say that. Tell them they are wonderful anyway. Just remember to appreciate them as a person. It is nice to tell them that you think they are a good baseball player, artist, or whatever they aspire to be. It is crucial that you tell them that they are a good person.

Our role as parents is to give our children love and wisdom. The more we can teach our children to be positive, the more they live a positive life. The more we teach children to approach the world from a place of love, the more we can teach our children to harness fear. This is the formula to equip our children with the tools necessary for a successful life experience.

Secret:
Five Factors That Determine the Course of Our Lives

Is there such a thing as bad luck or good luck? Or do things happen for a reason? If we assume things happen for a reason, there are two theories to consider regarding what we think of as good fortune, or luck. The first is that each person has different lessons to learn in this lifetime: some need the experience of how to handle good fortune; others are here to experience the opposite. The second theory is to understand our thoughts as energy, then consider that we are sending messages into the universe in the form of energy. What if the thoughts we sent out are answered? This energy may affect our interactions with destiny. Who knows, we might be able to think ourselves into luck or change our destiny. Give it a try, be optimistic, and expect good things to happen. Even if our energy doesn't change the universe, it will help us have a better attitude.

What happens during our life is determined by a combination of factors. They include: karmic debt, karmic reward, free will, the law of attraction and chosen lessons. While on Earth, free will and the Law of Attraction are the factors we have the greatest influence on. Karmic debt, karmic reward and the lessons we choose to master are influences we bring with us from the other side into this lifetime.

There are so many references to thoughts becoming things and the power of positive thinking that I couldn't begin to list them. Edgar Cayce articulated it in his work, and Rhonda Byrne discusses it at length in the book *The Secret*. One day when we go to the other side and have the opportunity for greater enlightenment regarding the events on Earth, it will all make perfect sense. For now, go with peace and work each day on being more positive. Positive attracts positive that is the Law of Attraction.

Secret:
We Have Karmic Encounters without Realizing It

It is quite foolish to think that the souls we do good deeds for and take care of are new to us. For example, I believe I have karmic links with many former students of mine. Whether it is Maria, Big Sue, Brian, Julia, Kim, Lisa, Big Greg, Neil, Seth, Phillip, Nicole, Marc, Laura, John, or any of the thousands of other kids who came my way, I believe that our interaction had a larger purpose.

An example of these karmic encounters is reflective of the story of David Brinker. My retelling of our first encounter is based on David's recall. Each year I worked at Hewlett High School, I would run a high school show called "Cabaret Night." It was a talent review that served as a fundraiser for the Laura Rosenberg Foundation. The Foundation raises funds to fight pediatric leukemia and support Happiness is Camping, a summer facility for children with cancer. In the early years that I ran the event there was a single show and not enough tickets. Parents and teachers would compete with students for a limited number of seats. David tells people the story that he came up to me as a sophomore unable to get a ticket to the show. David is not the type of person who will let a trivial matter such as not having a ticket stop him from moving forward. When David approached me about his predicament, I made him the same offer I made any student who wanted to see the show and could not get a ticket. I invited him to join the crew. I explained that we arrived at 8 A.M. and eleven hours later the gym was ready for the show. Unlike many students who had received the offer, David showed up and worked the entire day and even stayed through the close of the show to help us clean the gym. David told me that at the end of the night, I put my arm around him and said, "You are a great worker. Stick with me and you'll do great." That evening I didn't know that David was already a story of perseverance and success. David's father had passed away when he was six and left a family that also had a severely handicapped daughter. David's older brother had moved south as a successful physician.

David's mom took care of him as she visited her daughter in the nursing home and fought to make a living. If this wasn't enough, David developed diabetes and spent significant time in the hospital as a child. During the next two years, David worked with me as vice president and then president of the student council.

As a leader, David led a team of students that introduced and institutionalized changes that left Hewlett High School better for years to come. He learned the lesson that I taught student leaders; leave every place better than you found it. During David's senior year, as with many students, he fixated on attending one college as opposed to any of the other fine schools in the United States. David decided that Tufts University was his school. The only problem was that Tufts didn't have any room for David. He never took no for an answer and came to me with the name of an admissions counselor at Tufts. I called the gentleman, a man named Christopher Kim, and quickly developed a relationship with him as I presented the case for accepting David at Tufts. I told Christopher that if Tufts accepted David he would make the school better and become president of the student senate. At the end of our conversation, Christopher told me he would get back to me later that day. About an hour later my phone rang and Christopher asked me, "Do you really think this kid is that good?" I told him I was sure, and Christopher told me they would accept David at Tufts. Four years later, I attended David's graduation from Tufts as he left the school better and had indeed become president of the student senate.

I viewed our relationship as the satisfying experience a teacher has when he can help make a young person's life better. But karma and life are rarely simple. During the summer of 1992, my wife and son were in the hospital fighting for their lives. As I walked through the hospital lobby I looked up and saw David standing there. I inquired as to why he was there, and was told that he was doing an internship at the hospital during that summer. His presence could be considered a coincidence, or it could be an indication of a karmic connection that brought us together at my lowest moment. I do not consider my relationship with David to be an accident, but simply a karmic journey in which we encounter each other from time to time during this lifetime.

I do not believe that life is predetermined. There is a variety of crossroads we have during our lifetime in which a decision could take us in one direction or another. The people we encounter in our lives are not there by coincidence. I believe we know people from other lifetimes and we switch roles in a journey to gain experience from life to life. In various lifetimes a soul may be your best friend or your favorite teacher or your next-door neighbor. Part of the cosmic mystery is unraveling the relationships we have with other souls we encounter during our journey through life on this side. Remember each soul you encounter contributes to the growth of your soul through experience. Some of the worst people you meet may in fact be one of the most important experiences in this lifetime. Sometimes, I think God is laughing at us. Besides everything else, God appears to have a great sense of humor.

The concept of living out one's destiny is a familiar theme to sports fans. A ball hit poorly that falls in the right place has turned many a ballplayer into a hero as it sends the other side home in regret. Sports and unusual events go hand and hand. We have been trained to consider strange events as just coincidence. In 1999 the Yankees celebrated "Yogi Berra Day" by bringing back Don Larsen, the pitcher, who for one day in the 1956 World Series stood on top of the world, as he threw the only perfect game in Series history. Berra of course was the catcher who called the pitches that afternoon. Instead of the Hall of Fame catcher throwing out the first ball to start the game, the Yankees had Don Larsen throw the first ball to Yogi, an unusual way to open a ceremonial game, but fitting since the honoree was a catcher. It was in fact so unusual a way to open a game that Berra did not have a glove to catch Larsen's pitch. The honoree borrowed the catcher's glove of Yankee receiver Joe Girardi for the first pitch. Larsen then threw the pitch to Berra who caught the ball, received the cheers of the crowd and took the glove off and handed it back to Girardi.

With the glove fresh from the Hall of Famer's hand, Girardi proceeded to catch the third perfect game in Yankees' history as David Cone blanked the Expos. Two catchers wore the same glove that afternoon, one celebrating being the catcher in a historic perfect game, the other then became the catcher in a perfect game to be remembered in his own right. I say the third perfect game in Yankee history because the year before, David Wells threw the second perfect game in Yankee history. It happens Don Larsen was also in the ballpark for that game. Wells and Larson even graduated from the same high school in San Diego. Coincidence or a karmic crossroad?

Following Berra's playing career he managed the Yankees to the World Series. Following Girardi's playing career he managed the Yankees to the World Series. And so on, and so on...

Secret:
Karmic Debt and the Law of Attraction

Edgar Cayce described Karma as memory, usually from another lifetime. We do many good things in our lives, but from time to time, we do not do the right thing. It is important we understand that our soul needs to learn why something we did was wrong. Learning this lesson is fulfilling a karmic debt. The universe does not punish, but it must educate the soul. If the soul can learn the inherent wrong of an act, it may not have to experience it. However, the best teacher is experience. So we do live our lives with the need to pay a karmic debt. The fewer hurtful things we do in a life, the fewer lessons we will have in the next lifetime.

Those who have learned about the Law of Attraction through works such as *The Secret* and *The Power of Positive Thinking* are often disappointed when they apply positive thinking to their lives and it doesn't seem to change their world. They may believe the law is faulty, or it is may be that they do not know how to apply positive thinking and are making some sort of mistake. What they might not recognize is that the bad experience is one that the soul chose to learn as a karmic lesson. They forget that there is more than one law at work in the universe and we need to consider how two cosmic forces complement each other. The universe may be receiving conflicting signals from the soul.

Karmic debt from previous lifetimes is not a punishment. It is, rather, a learning lesson that we have to master based on hurtful choices we have made in other lifetimes. It is a memory of something we did wrong and need to learn not to do again. Part of our present life experience is trying to master lessons from prior lifetimes that we failed to learn. Therefore, if we find that life isn't changing as expected when we apply the Law of Attraction through positive thinking, what might be happening is that karmic debt is causing our soul to subliminally block the change.

When we meet our karmic debt or we learn our life lesson, we are released from the situation that we have found unpleasant. Debt met, lesson learned, happiness awaits. And if we want we can apply the positive effects of the Law of Attraction.

In a karmic sense, it is all good in the long run. Our soul eventually returns back to the other side and can again be in a state of joy. However, in each individual lifetime, we might experience hardship that seems unfair or unbearable. Sometimes the hardship is a karmic *lesson* to be learned through experience. Sometimes it is karmic *debt*—learning for the soul that was purposely made to happen in this lifetime based on a choice we should have made differently in a prior lifetime.

Secret:
Although We Come to Earth with Chosen Lessons to Learn, We Live with Free Will

According to the American prophet, Edgar Cayce, the future is never completely set. God has set up the world with free choice. The final choice of what is to happen remains with us. We need to make our life choices wisely because ultimately we are responsible for our experience. One of the most difficult bridges to cross on Earth is accepting the fact that we each create our own life experience. That is the way God wanted it, and that is the way it is.

Prior to our birth, we choose particular lessons to learn during our lifetime. However, the way we experience life lessons is flexible and open to the choices we make during our lifetime. We may also want to consider that we may fail to accomplish the learning we were pursuing when we came here. That is fine since we will simply learn something else as all experiences for the soul are meaningful. Since all knowledge is helpful to the soul's maturation, the experience of life can only be positive regardless of the lessons we have learned through our experience. If we fail to get the entire experience that we desired, we can simply choose to learn it again in another lifetime.

We have come to Earth to learn major lessons that we designated prior to our arrival. We may have chosen to experience lessons on relationships, perseverance, strength, and sometimes even loss and pain. How we learn these lessons is most likely not revealed to the soul prior to the birth here on Earth. If the soul knew exactly what was to happen, it would likely alter the learning process and compromise the experience. The research of Hans Holzer indicates that we actually go through a shower prior to our birth in which our memories of past lives become hidden from our consciousness. Just like any shower, some parts do not get completely clean, so for some, memories of past lives linger.

So if one considers whether the events of life are predetermined, the answer is a little yes and a little no. We do plan for our soul to learn certain lessons and explore particular areas. For example, experiencing relationships or learning about loss may be a karmic choice. But I do believe that the choices we make in our life determine the exact course of experience and often take our experience in very interesting directions that we had not considered prior to our arrival on Earth.

Secret:
Time is An Illusion

When we consider that life is about learning lessons through experience, a fair question arises for our Creator. Why can't you just give us the experience quickly, say, in a day or so? Many of our Earthly experiences are very painful and extending the lesson seems cruel.

What if we did get an answer from the Creator and it was something that we completely didn't expect? That being, the lesson is very quick, it just seems to be taking place over an extended period of time. For the reality is, time is not real: it is a creation.

Albert Einstein stated that the only reason for time is so that everything doesn't happen at once. In other words, time is a creation that allows our experience to occur in an orderly environment. Without time, everything would sort of bang into each other. Einstein's Theory of Relativity pointed out that time can actually be changed by speed and direction of a travelling object. Experiments have proven him to be right. Time is not a constant, it can be altered.

The understanding of time is helpful to understanding the Secrets of Life and Death. There is no time as we know it on the other side, therefore souls exist differently. On our side, our perception of our experiences change once we recognize that it all may be happening in a flash of a second in the perspective of the Universe. As we presently consider our lives, we perceive our lives are happening over many decades and of course decades are extended periods of time.

The events of our lives occur in a linear fashion because we think in terms of events only occurring one following another. The idea of linear time means one event happens before another in a straight line. But since time is nonlinear, we can't really be sure of anything with certainty. Can all the events of our lifetime be happening almost simultaneously, based on the exercise of our free will? One event has to follow another because of the fact that if we make one decision our life will go in one direction, and if we make another, we live a different life. For example, among the many choices in our lives is the choice of the college we attend. Let's say instead of the choice you made regarding the college to attend, for whatever reason you chose to attend a different school. Everyone you meet and the events of life would have been different over the next four years. In fact many, many factors in your life would change from the moment you made the different choice.

Events and occurrences in our world may be taking place at a blinding speed. In fact everything may be slowed down in our mind as we live in a physical universe, but the reality may not be as we perceive it. 70 or 80 years in our lifetime may take place in an instant to the other side. So as we consider that we leave our home on the other side to come to Earth to learn lessons, we may actually be only gone for the time it takes to blink an eye...or not really gone at all.

Secret:
The Book of Life and Alternative Lives

The plotline of the unique television show *"Fringe"* is based on the concept of parallel universes. More specifically, in the show there is another universe in which we (our counterpart self) live a slightly different life based on the different choices we make in the parallel universe. For example, when we think of decisions we have made at the crossroads of our life, we never know what would have happened if we made the other choice. What if, we existed in multiple universes and we made the other choice in the parallel universe. Interesting stuff to consider, but what if it is not science fiction?

Edgar Cayce, in many of his readings, talked about the Akashic Records, a universal archive of every thought, every deed, and every feeling that every soul on Earth has had or committed throughout all time. (It is also called the Book of Life, and like the concept described in the Bible, it records the complete history of every soul that has ever lived. However, the Akashic Records is far broader in scope in that its purpose is not just for determining whether a soul gains entry into heaven but is a way for all souls to be connected to each other.) Cayce, in one particular reading, described how the Akashic Records had a record of what would have happened to him if he had married a different woman, someone who he was close to as a young man but not his actual wife in this earthly life. The records had the results of the different life that he would have lived based on a different choice.

Regarding his ability to speak about the unknown, Cayce said that when he entered a trance, he went to the Akashic Records and a man was there who always knew what information he needed. Of course, the readings were often about people and not the organization of the universe.

However, for fun, let's consider if in another universe you exist with a different life experience based on the choices you have made—let's say an Oprah Winfrey in a different universe. Her remarkable biography tells how she overcame an environment of abuse and an unstable home life in her early teen years. She turned her life around after she moved into a secure home that got her to exercise the discipline she needed to excel in her studies. But imagine another world in which she did not have the chance to change her life and continued as a young person to make self-destructive decisions? In that universe, she would have a very different experience, maybe a hard life on the streets and her soul would have learned very different things. What's more it is highly unlikely that we would have a hugely successful talk show host who has the celebrity to influence so many around the world.

There is an interesting question for those familiar with the writings of Edgar Cayce. What if the Book of Life was not reporting the life story of what would have happened if he had made a different decision? What if the Book was not depicting a what-if, but in fact reporting his life in a parallel universe?

If our soul may be learning multiple lessons at the same time, we might ask why just two universes? Why not numerous universes in which we have slightly different experiences in each so that our exercise of free will creates dramatically different life experiences. After all, if we can conceive of and think about reincarnation, why not parallel incarnation? Remember, the choices we make determine the life we live. Different choices—different life. Fun to think about.

Secret:
There Is a Philosophy about How to Approach Each Day

The Latin phrase, *carpe diem* is a two-word tutorial on daily life. It literally means "seize the day," but what it implies is "make it special." If there is a formula involved, it would be this: each day do something for others, do something for oneself, learn something new, touch base with friends, and tell someone how much they are appreciated and loved.

Tomorrow is promised to no one—seize the day. If this were the last day of your life, what kind of things would you like to do with it? Would you tell your loved ones how important they are to you? Would you watch the sunset? Play with your kids? While it is important to find work that is valuable and has purpose, it is equally important to find joy in each day. Life habits are just that, if you get into a pattern to put off joy until tomorrow, you will eventually run out of tomorrows.

The funny thing about the way we raise our children is that we concern ourselves primarily with how they can be economically secure, and we just assume their happiness will follow. It is culturally ingrained that we think happiness accompanies economic security. Economic security is important, but it in no measure guarantees happiness. My grandmother used to say, "As long as you have your health." Certainly at the time, the words she said were lost on my young mind. But as I got older, I remembered her words. She had obviously planted the seed. Discussions about seizing the day remind me of the story I heard about a couple who were both actors. When they were young and struggling in their careers, he bought her a bag of peanuts and enclosed a note on which he had written, "I wish they were a bag of diamonds." As the years passed, the actors became very successful and wealthy. In old age he bought her a bag of diamonds and put a note inside that read, "I wish they were a bag of peanuts." Happiness doesn't come automatically with economic security; the struggle is part of the fun. Carpe diem!

Secret:
How We Get Released from Bad Situations

At one time or another, when times have been tough, many of us have looked up at the sky and asked, Why me? And when things aren't good for an extended period of time, we wonder why they are bad for so long. It is at these times that it is helpful to remember that events in our lives do not happen by chance. Situations arise as a result of the way we think, the life we lead, and the choices we make. However, this lifetime is also affected by what our soul desires to learn, and that determines, in part, what comes into this physical plain. When we are in a bad situation, we can take actions that will offer a number of remedies, virtually all involving a change in the way we think, and therefore a changed vibrational pattern. That means every time we want to change our life and be released from a bad situation, we must first have mastered the lesson that was given to us by the situation.

My friend Joan was working for a boss from hell and did not seem to be able to find a way out. When she interviewed for other jobs, fate stepped in and denied her a release from her bad situation. One day she called me excited to tell me that she had run into someone she knew who had just offered her another job. I asked Joan what had changed. Confused, she said "What do you mean?" I asked her what happened the days before she had run into the person who offered her the new job. She replied, "Well the day before, my boss was so disgusting and abusive, I had gone home and looked up and said to God, 'Why is this happening to me? I am too good a person for this.'" I laughed and I said to Joan, "So you had learned your lesson." Again confused, she said "What was my lesson?" I explained, "Your lesson was to love yourself the way others love you. Once you told the universe you are worthy of love and you knew it, you were released from the abuse."

Our soul takes into account karmic debts, karmic rewards, and karmic lessons from other lifetimes. Life experiences, including bad situations, are chances for the soul to learn its lessons. So, if things aren't going the way we want, we have to figure out what the lesson is that we have to learn from the situation. Figure out the lesson, master it, and you will be released. Fail to master the lesson and you may get to another place or a new relationship, but you can be sure that the life lesson will follow you until the lesson has been mastered

In Summary

The Last Word About Life Goes to Those Who Come Back after a Short Trip Away from Life

As discussed earlier, Psychiatrist Raymond A. Moody M.D. devoted his career to interviewing over two thousand people who had an after-life experience or were pronounced dead by medical practitioners, but somehow returned to life. The consistency of the message regarding the afterlife experience from all these people is striking—and the descriptions breathtaking. Each person interviewed depicted similar although not exact situations in which they were drawn into a tunnel from which they could see a bright light at the end. As they emerged from the tunnel and came into the light the common report is they felt they were greeted by a presence of pure love and acceptance. That is the same love and acceptance that created our essence. Each person felt a sense of peace and joy along with the love that was at least equal to or greater than anything they had felt on Earth. They also reported that they could take in a panoramic view of every event that had taken place in their lifetime. Additionally, they could see the ripple effect, good and bad, of every action of their lives.

It seems counterintuitive to those of us still in earthly life, but the great events of these people's lifetimes were not the key focus during the after-life review of events. It was the simple acts of kindness and love that each individual had engaged in during their lives that were more important. Invariably people reported that they were sent back to Earth because they had not completed their mission in regard to affecting others, though they said that they would have preferred to stay on the other side.

As previously mentioned, a documentary about Moody's work includes an interview with a person who had committed suicide and decided to return to life on Earth. According to her account, she was told that she could stay on the other side or she could return to Earth, but she was given conditions. If she stayed on the other side, in her next lifetime on Earth, she would have to relive the same experiences up to the point of her suicide to see if her soul had learned to make another choice. She chose to come back.

Some scientists argue that these experiences are simply the recollection of the brain shutting down during a phase when the body is clinically dead but still in the process of dying. Dr. Moody effectively refutes this argument by pointing to numerous situations in which those who have passed over and returned have given information that could not be explained with that theory. For example, two of the people Dr. Moody interviewed in the documentary provided testimony consistent with the soul leaving the body. In one story, Moody recounts that a nurse he had interviewed reported that a woman who had died and returned to life told her of a shoe on a ledge outside the fifth floor of the hospital. When asked further about it, the woman told the nurse she saw it as her body went toward the tunnel. The shoe did turn out to be on the ledge. Providing first-hand testimony in the documentary film, another woman who had died and returned from the other side stated that her brother-in-law had told someone that he wasn't able to go on a trip because his sister-in-law had just "kicked the bucket." The same woman traveled to her sisters' and saw what they were doing at that moment. Upon returning to life and speaking to her sisters and brother-in-law, she was able to confirm that the observations she made at that time were completely accurate. Her brother-in-law was quite embarrassed to admit that he had made a disrespectful comment. The evidence was overwhelming that she had in fact left her body and witnessed events before heading to the light. Also, in some cases the brain was dead for a significant amount of time and there would be no way to have a thought process.

A short statement compiled from over two thousand cases of people who had experienced (even if for a brief time) life after life sums up what they learned: "It is all about love." We are here on Earth to learn how to love and accept each other in the way God loves us and accepts us.

Love is the *Secret of Life*. Love is the *Secret of Death*. Love is the *Secret of Joy, Peace and Meaning While on Earth*. My own personal journey and search for answers has taken me through situations from the simple to the complex, the painful to the wonderful. My explorations have resulted in the simplest answer: Love is what we are here to learn; love is what we return to; love is the secret to joy, peace and meaning while on Earth.

The final word is the word of the creator—*love*.

SHEARISMS

1. The most powerful force in the universe is love.

2. We never die as our life continues in another dimension.

3. Life events are a combination of free will, karmic debt, karmic reward, chosen lessons, and the Law of Attraction.

4. Earth is a university designed for our soul to learn through experience.

5. Life in heaven is real. Life on Earth is an experience for the soul—it is real *and* it is an illusion. We are spiritual beings having a physical manifestation.

6. When we return to heaven, we are thankful for all the experiences that helped our soul progress for life's purpose is soul progression.

7. Following our stay on Earth we undergo a life review with a full panoramic view of our actions and their effects on others.

8. Evil is an outgrowth of fear. It is defeated by being brought into the light of love and forgiveness.

9. We frequently get messages from loved ones on the other side of life; we have been trained to not believe the source.

10. We create our life experience by what we choose to focus on.

11. Set up the game of life so that you win.

12. Events in the world are an outgrowth of the collective consciousness of humankind.

13. Forgiveness frees our own soul.

14. People who do terrible things have not lost their soul; it has receded into their body.

15. Hell is when an entity is separated from God.

16. Tolerance and acceptance of the difference in others is crucial to our survival.

17. Human history is filled with people whose best days came after they thought all was lost.

18. Energy thieves need to draw energy from others to live.

19. We can't fool God.

20. To be happy we must live in a state of appreciation and gratitude.

21. In order to have a happy life, we must be involved in meaningful work.

22. Because God provided us with free will, even he doesn't know the exact outcome of this lifetime for each of us. Ultimately, it is up to us.

23. For many, the important life lesson is to learn to love and forgive oneself.

24. To the creator, our mistakes are like a child's mistakes are to a parent: We get corrected and forgiven.

25. We are at our best when we care for each other.

GO WITH PEACE!

Acknowledgements

There are always many more people involved in a major enterprise than is immediately apparent. This book would not have been completed without the support of my family who encouraged me to keep going in pursuit of truth; and my friends and acquaintances who have patiently heard me talking about this book since Moses was a teenager. I also owe a debt to the work of some very enlightened souls, who have worked to educate our world. They include but are not limited to: Edgar Cayce, Bryan Weiss, Raymond Moody, Neil Donald Walsh, Rhonda Byrne, Glen Dove, Gary Schwartz, Steve Friedman and many, many more. And, finally, I want to acknowledge the individuals who will read *The Secrets of Life and Death* and spread the message that life is eternal, has meaning and that everything we do in life matters.

19510081R00109

Made in the USA
Lexington, KY
21 December 2012